creating dynamic
multimedia
presentations

Using Microsoft PowerPoint®

Carol M. Lehman
Mississippi State University

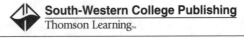

South-Western College Publishing
Thomson Learning™

Australia • Canada • Denmark • Japan • Mexico • New Zealand • Philippines
Puerto Rico • Singapore • South Africa • Spain • United Kingdom • United States

Creating Dynamic Multimedia Presentations Using MicroSoft PowerPoint
by Carol M. Lehman

Publisher: Dave Shaut
Acquisitions Editor: Pamela M. Person
Production Editor: Kelly Keeler
Manufacturing Coordinator: Sandee Milewski
Production House: Susan Peterson
Printer: Mazer Corporation

Printed in the United States of America
1 2 3 4 5 02 01 00 99

For more information contact South-Western College Publishing, 5101 Madison Road,
Cincinnati, Ohio, 45227 or find us on the Internet at http://www.swcollege.com
For permission to use material from this text or product,contact us by
• **telephone: 1-800-730-2214**
• **fax: 1-800-730-2215**
• **web: http://www.thomsonrights.com**

ISBN 0-324-02537-8

This book is printed on acid-free paper.

BRIEF CONTENTS

CONTENTS

Preface

Throughout your career, you will be judged by the effectiveness with which you communicate orally in your daily activities. You might make a presentation to your peers in committee work, to subordinates as a part of a training or information program, or a formal presentation to senior management or a client. In each case your reputation is on the line. When you are effective, you gain status and earn respect. You find managing others easier, and you become promotable to increasingly higher levels.

The basics of preparing an effective presentation have not changed with the advent of computer graphics and multimedia packages. No innovative technological tool can substitute for the ability to determine a purpose that meets an audience's needs, relate ideas clearly and effectively, and be sincere and responsive to the audience. Today's managers must focus on fundamental communication skills while using technology to enhance each phase of the presentation process: designing top-notch presentation support tools (slide show, overheads, audience handouts), rehearsing effectively, and delivering the presentation in a seamless, effortless manner.

For this reason, this book goes beyond the simple how-to manual for learning to create simple PowerPoint presentations using standard presentation designs and consisting of dense, countless bulleted lists and other bland, dull designs. In ten short projects, you will

- Master the full functionality of Microsoft PowerPoint 2000 or PowerPoint '97.

- Apply presentation design guidelines to develop creative, dynamic, and highly effective business presentations that will set you apart from the typical presenter.

- Master techniques for delivering the presentation so the audience's attention remains focused on you, the speaker — not the technology.

While building 28 slides using numerous creative design techniques, you will encounter feature boxes that provide supplemental information related to four important presentation areas:

- **Designer's Pointers** —basic slide design guidelines that lead to the development of compelling slides that communicate ideas effectively and involve the audience in the message.

- **Speaker's Tips** — suggestions for using a specific PowerPoint feature and design technique to deliver a presentation in an effective manner.

- **FYI** — tidbits of information related to multimedia development that reaches beyond the operation of PowerPoint (e.g., locating multimedia objects on the Internet, efficient method for completing a design technique).

- **Trouble Shooting Tips** — detailed assistance with PowerPoint or Windows-related operations; problems the author has anticipated as a result of extensive training experience.

After you learn to start PowerPoint, apply a standard presentation design, and a standard slide layout, you will create a couple basic slides and then advance directly into applying creative techniques. To expedite your mastery of these powerful skills, the text walks you through a thoughtful critique of what is referred to as an original slide — one that a novice might create. You spend your valuable time creating an enhanced slide that (a) corrects violations in basic slide design guidelines; (b) applies fundamental communication skills, such as aiding the speaker by clarifying or emphasizing a point or building coherence within the presentation; or (c) incorporates a more appealing design. Specific skills you will learn include:

- Creating a basic presentation including a title slide, a bulleted list, simple clip art, slide transitions, and custom animation.
- Using drawing tools, clip art, WordArt, photographs, and sound to enhance a basic presentation.

- Designing a custom template to fit the needs of a specific audience or topic.
- Adding creative animation techniques including automatic timings, hide after mouse click, and hide after animation techniques.
- Creating compelling tables and graphs that clarify and reinforce potentially overwhelming numerical data.
- Designing coherence devices that assist an audience in moving smoothing through the organizational structure of a presentation.
- Using the speller, style checker, and the rehearse timings feature to identify improvements while rehearsing the delivery of a presentation.
- Creating useful speaker's notes and professional audience handouts that increase the overall impact of a speaker's delivery.
- Incorporating techniques that make a presentation interactive; for example, hidden slides and hyperlinks that add flexibility to the order in which slides can be projected and other design techniques that foster audience involvement.
- Compressing large presentations so they can be transported to other computers.

The time devoted to completing this textbook will yield positive results as you seek to become an effective speaker in the competitive 21st century. Strive to design dynamic PowerPoint presentations that set you apart from the typical presenter. Focus on timeless communication skills that ensure your presentation connects with your audience and achieves the goals you have established for that group — regardless of the presentation media you choose. Lastly, incorporate design features that assist you in delivering a slide show in an effortless, seamless manner. Practice until the technology is virtually transparent, positioned in the background to serve as your supporting cast. In this performance you are the star, and you will reap the benefits gained from honing your presentation skills to meet the high expectations of today's audiences.

Project 1
Getting Started with PowerPoint

Learning Objectives
➤ Start PowerPoint and understand the parts of the PowerPoint screen
➤ Apply a template to a new and an existing presentation.
➤ Create a title slide and bulleted list using an AutoLayout.
➤ Add a new placeholder to customize PowerPoint's AutoLayout to fit a presentation.
➤ Change the appearance of text.
➤ Save a presentation.
➤ Work with PowerPoint in normal. slide sorter. and slide show views.

Understanding PowerPoint
PowerPoint is a graphics software program that allows you to create visual aids for supporting a speaker's presentation. The presentation can be projected on a screen using projection equipment or printed as transparencies acetates.

Terms

PowerPoint presentation	A collection of slides relating to the same topic.
Slide	Comparable to pages of a word processing document or sheets within a notebook file. Slides are added individually to a presentation as the presentation is built.

Starting PowerPoint
1 Double click the PowerPoint icon (or Click **Start, Programs, Office 2000, PowerPoint**). The startup dialog box appears.
2 Note three options for creating a new presentation and two options for opening an existing presentation.
3 Click **Design Template** to start PowerPoint. Then continue reading on the next page.

PowerPoint 97 users: Click **Start, Programs, Office 97, PowerPoint**.

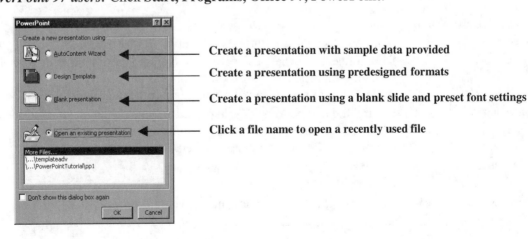

Understanding the PowerPoint Window

Study the following diagram and terms that identify and explain the various elements of the PowerPoint screen and presentation window.

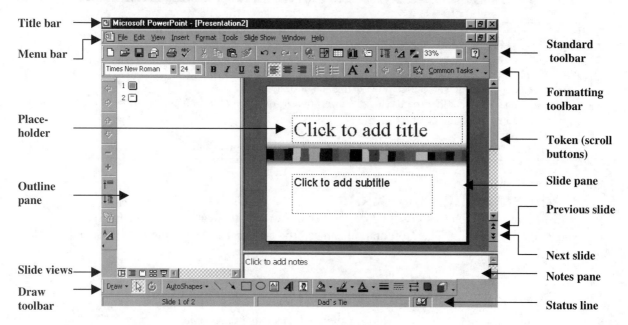

PowerPoint 97 users: The slide pane will occupy the entire window.

Terms

Screen Parts

Title Bar	Identifies that PowerPoint is running and displays file name.
Menu Bar	Provides pop-down menus from which features can be accessed.
Standard Toolbar	Gives quick access to the most frequently used file functions.
Formatting Toolbar	Provides buttons for changing fonts, sizes, attributes, and color.
Draw Toolbar	Provides buttons for inserting text or quick graphics.

Presentation Window

Slide	Displays placeholders for text and graphics to be inserted.
Placeholder	Dotted-line boxes that designate the location on a slide in which titles, text, art, graphics, charts, and others objects are placed.
Text object	A term used to describe text in a text box (often a graphic object).
View buttons	Control the number of slides displayed and the display layout (slide, outline, slide sorter, notes page, and slide show).
Status bar	Contains slide # and template selected.
Previous slide	Displays the previous slide.
Next slide	Displays the next slide.
Horizontal and vertical token (scroll buttons)	Moves the text in the window up, down, left, or right.

Understanding Templates

PowerPoint provides an extensive library of predesigned templates created by professional graphic artists. These templates include formatting for color, fonts, bullets, graphics, and other formatting that makes creating a basic presentation simple.

Selecting and Applying a Template to a New Presentation

1   Click **Design Template** (from the opening menu).
   Note: You completed this step already to allow you to review the PowerPoint window.
2   Click the **Design Templates** tab.
3   Point to a template and click to view the template in the lower right corner.
4   Click **OK** to apply the template to your presentation. You may also double click on the template to select it.

   PowerPoint 97 users: Click **Template** from the opening menu and the **Presentation Designs** tab.

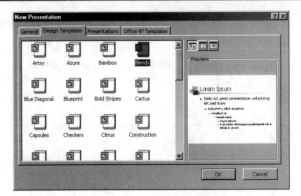

Selecting and Applying a Template to an Existing Presentation

You will select a different template for the presentation you've just opened in this section. Note that only **one** template can be applied to a single presentation file.

1   Click **Format, Apply Design Template** (or **Template** button on the Formatting Toolbar).

The Presentation Template dialog box displays a list of available options:

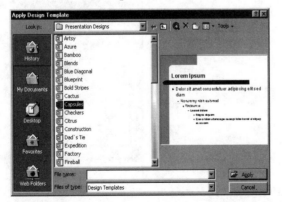

2   Click a **file name** in the File Name dialog box. Preview the template displayed at the right.
3   Press **OK** when you locate the desired template.
4   Proceed to the next section.

FYI

Become familiar with other sources of presentation designs (templates) that will create exactly the mood you wish to convey.

* Click **Help, Microsoft on the Web** and download new templates from Microsoft's web site. New templates are added to this site regularly. *You will learn more about locating template, images, and sound from the Internet in Project 3.*
* Select a template from the **AutoContent Wizard** (option on PowerPoint's opening menu). Supply your own text.
* Select a template from the "Web Designs" tab if you plan to post your presentation to the Internet.

Creating a Title Slide and a Simple Bulleted List

PowerPoint provides the basic structure for numerous slide layouts, and you simply click in the designated area (placeholder) and input text and graphics. These layouts allow you to create a slide show with consistent, professional appearance quickly and easily. Additionally, you can customize these layouts to fit the content of your presentation.

Creating a Title Slide

Directions: Follow the instructions to complete Slide 1 (shown at right).

1   Be certain the New Slide Dialog Box is displayed. This box shows the predesigned slide layouts.

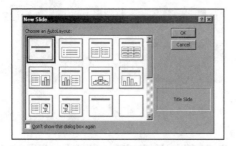

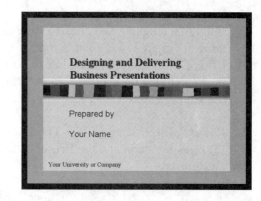

2   Note the border surrounds the first slide layout and a description, "Title Slide" appears in the bottom right corner. When you click the desired layout, a brief description appears in the bottom right corner of the screen.

3   Click the second slide layout and note the description is "Bulleted Slide." Become familiar with the layouts by clicking other layouts. Notice the graphics on each layout provide visual cues to the nature of each layout. Click the down arrow and move down to reveal all 32 slide layouts.

4   Select **Title** as the slide layout.

5   Click in the title placeholder and key the title.

6   Click in the sub-title placeholder and key the sub-title.

7   Continue developing this slide in the next section.

Working with New Placeholders

Directions: Follow the instructions to continue building Slide 1 (shown at right).

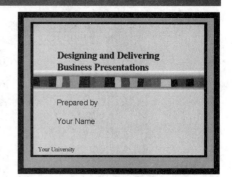

Create a New Placeholder

1   Click the **Text** button on the Draw Toolbar.

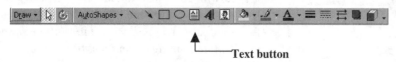

Text button

2   Position the mouse pointer anywhere on the slide. Click and hold the left mouse button as you drag down and to the right. A border representing the placeholder appears.

3   Key the text in the placeholder: **your company/university.**

Reposition a Placeholder

4   Click once anywhere within the placeholder. A diagonal border with small black sizing boxes [handles] between and on the corners of the highlighted border appears.

5   Point at the horizontal placeholder and click again to select the placeholder. The horizontal border between the sizing handles are now shaded.

6   Move the mouse pointer directly between any two handles until the mouse pointer turns into a four-headed arrow.

7   Click and hold the left mouse and drag the placeholder to its new location at the bottom left of the slide. Note the icon attached to the mouse pointer indicates you are moving text.

FYI

Hold down the Shift key and drag a corner sizing handle to change the width and the height proportionally. This technique is especially useful when resizing clip art, photos, and charts.

8   Release the mouse button when the placeholder is in position.

9   Click anywhere outside the placeholder to deselect the placeholder.

Resize a Placeholder

10   Point to the *sizing handle* on the right side of the placeholder and drag to the right until the text fits on one line.

Delete a Placeholder

11   Select the placeholder and press **Delete**.

12   Click the **Undo** button (curved arrow pointing left) on the Standard toolbar to restore the placeholder.

Edit Text in a Placeholder

As you edit the appearance of the text in the placeholder you created, you will become familiar with the numerous ways text can be enhanced to produce a creative design. In Project 4 you will learn to edit the Master Slide to change the appearance of standard design elements such as the slide title and bulleted lists.

13   Highlight the text to be edited. Click the **Bold** button on the Formatting toolbar.

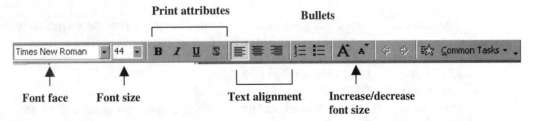

Print attributes   Bullets

Font face   Font size   Text alignment   Increase/decrease font size

FYI

The placeholder you are editing is referred to as *specimen placeholder*. In other words, it is one of a kind in a presentation. However, be sure to copy this same format to similar placeholders you add to other slides. To change the appearance of standard design elements such as the slide title or a bulleted list, edit the Master Slide. An edit made on the Master Slide will change the appearance of all slides, eliminating the need to edit each slide individually.

14 Highlight the text to be edited. Click **Format, Font**.

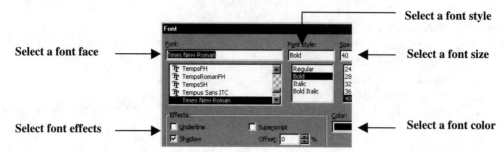

15 Select a new font by clicking the down arrow in the Font Face box.

16 Change the font size to **14 points** by clicking the down arrow in the Font Size box.

17 Change the text color by clicking the down arrow in the Color box and selecting a color from the following menu.

Select a color complimentary with your template background but has high contrast so the audience can read the text easily.

18 Study other changes that can be made from the Font dialog box (shown above).

19 Make the following changes by clicking icons on the Draw Toolbar: (a) Add a border around the placeholder that is a dashed line 1 point wide, and (b) select a border color complimentary with your template background.

20 Study other changes that can be made from the Draw toolbar

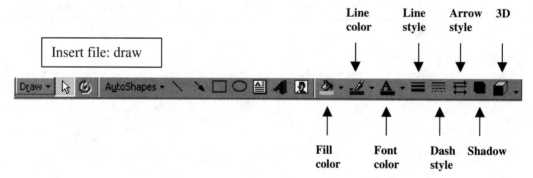

—	*Font color:*	Color of text. Several colors that are complimentary with the presentation displayed. Click **More Fill Colors** to select a different color.
—	*Fill color:*	Solid color behind the placeholder
—	*Line color:*	Line around the placeholder
—	*Line style:*	Width of line around the placeholder
—	*Dash style*:	Style of line around the placeholder (solid, dashed, dotted, etc.)
—	*Arrow style*:	Style of arrow
—	*Shadow*:	Several shadow effects
—	*3D effect*:	Several 3D effects

Trouble Shooting Tip

Click **View, Toolbars** and note the list includes check marks before the toolbars that are currently displayed. Click in front of Common Tasks to remove the check mark; note this toolbar is no longer displayed on the screen. Click **View Toolbars, Picture** again to redisplay the toolbar.

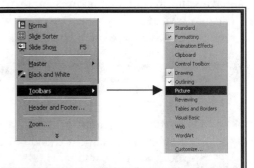

Creating a Bulleted List

Directions: Follow the instructions to build Slide 2 (shown at right).

1 Click **New Slide** on the Standard toolbar or the Common Tasks toolbar.
2 Click **Slide Layout**.
3 Click **Bulleted List** and click **OK** (or double click **Bulleted List.**)
4 Click the title placeholder and key the slide title (shown at right).
5 Click in the bulleted list placeholder and key the text for the first bulleted item.
6 Press **Enter**.
7 Key the remaining bulleted items.

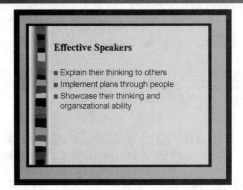

Designer's Pointer

Follow these capitalization rules when building slides:

1. **Use initial caps in slide titles.** Lowercase words are easier to read than UPPERCASE WORDS. Uppercase was used to emphasize ideas in the age of the typewriter. Today emphasis is added with bold and shadow effects, changes to font face, size, and color, etc.

2. **Capitalize only the first word in bulleted lists.** This style allows viewers to scan a line of text and comprehend ideas quickly. A viewer's eyes move up and down with initial caps (first word and important words capitalized), which creates a wave effect that is distracting and decreases readability.

Saving and Closing a Presentation and Exiting PowerPoint

Save your presentation on the hard drive or a floppy so you can open and edit the file at a later time. Plan to save after you have created each slide to prevent losing data if power is interrupted to your computer. Save more often when building slides that require a great deal of time and effort.

Saving a Presentation

1 Click **File, Save As.**
2 Click in the Save In box and key a drive designation (e.g., drive).
3 Click in the File Name box and key **Speak** as the file name.
4 Click **Save.**

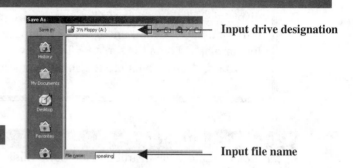

Input drive designation

Input file name

Closing a Presentation

1 Click **File, Close**.
The file is no longer in your computer's memory but can be reopened for later use.

Exiting PowerPoint

1 Click **File, Exit.**

Opening an Existing Presentation

You can open a presentation that has been saved on the hard drive or a floppy for making revisions.

Opening an Existing Presentation When Starting PowerPoint

To complete this activity, you must have exited PowerPoint.
1 Restart PowerPoint, (**Start, Programs, Office 2000, PowerPoint**).
2 Click **Open an existing presentation** from the startup dialog box.
3 Check to see if **Speak** is listed in the recently used files.
— If **Speak** is in the list, click the file name and **OK**.
— If **Speak** is not in the list, click in the Look-In box and key a drive destination (e.g., a: drive). Click **Open**.

List of recently used files

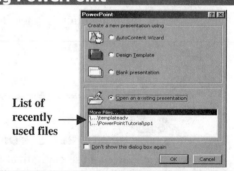

Opening an Existing Presentation With PowerPoint Started

When PowerPoint is already started, follow these steps to open an existing presentation:
1 Click **File, Open**. The Open dialog box appears.
2 Click in the Look-In box and key a drive destination (e.g., a: drive).
3 Check to see if **Speak** is listed in the recently used files:
— If Speak is in the list, click the file name, and **OK**.
— If Speak is not in the list, click in the **Look-In** box and key a drive destination (e.g., a: drive). Click **Open**.

List of recently opened files

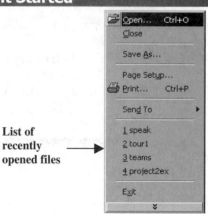

Viewing a Presentation

View buttons control the number of slides displayed and the display layout. The view buttons (normal, slide, slide sorter, and slide show) are located at the bottom left side of the screen.

Normal View

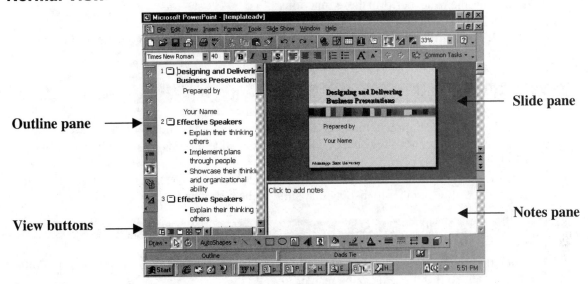

The normal view combines the outline, slide, and notes views so you can work in these sections of your presentation in one view. You can adjust the size of different panes by dragging the borders.

OUTLINE PANE

Outline view displays only title and body text for slides. This view facilitates organizing ideas in a presentation and is the most efficient view for entering text for numerous slides.

To move slides in the outline view:
Click the icon to the right of the slide number and drag the slide to the desired position. Drop the slide by releasing the left mouse button (drag and drop procedure).

To delete slides in the normal view view:
Click the icon of a slide. All text is highlighted. Press **Delete**. Click **Yes** at the confirmation prompt.

SLIDE PANE

The slide pane displays a single slide with text and graphics. This default view is useful for entering text and graphics.

NOTES PANE

The Notes Pane provides space below the slide pane where text and graphics can be inserted. The pane can be used for (a) inputting notes to prompt the speaker's next point and (b) inputting cues to aid a projectionist advancing the slide show for a speaker, and (c) recording ideas for further slide design.

PowerPoint 97 Users: The Normal View is a new software feature that allows you to see a slide in three views (slide, notes pages, and outline) on one screen. When using PowerPoint 97, change to the desired view rather than clicking within the panes.

Moving and Deleting Slides in Normal View

Click the Normal view from the status line at the bottom of the screen or click **View, Normal** from the pop-down list. The view button of the selected view will appear depressed slightly.

1 Switch to Normal view.
2 In the outline pane, perform these functions:
   (a) Delete a slide and Undo to restore it.
   (b) Move the title slide to a new location and then return it to its original position.
   (c) Change a word on a slide.

Moving Within a Presentation in Normal View

1 Display Slide 1 in Normal view and click in the slide pane.
2 Use the next slide button to move to Slide 2 and the previous slide button to move back to Slide 1.
3 Use the token (located above the previous and next slide buttons) to move between Slides 1 and 2.
4 Click in the outline pane.
5 Use the up and down arrow keys to display a slide number. Then, click the highlighted icon to the right of the slide number to display that slide in the slide pane.

Inputting Text in the Notes Pane

1 Click inside the notes pane.
2 Click the right arrow to the right of **Zoom** (located at the right side of the Standard Toolbar). Select 66% so that the text can be read easily.

Zoom

3 Key the text (key a couple sentences that you might use to introduce this topic).
4 Select all the text in the placeholder by holding **Ctrl and pressing A (Ctl-A)**.
5 Increase the font size to at least 14 points so that the notes can be read easily in a darkened room (adjust to a speaker's needs for a specific presentation).

Resize the Notes Pane to Allow Additional Space for Notes

1 Point to the top border of the notes pane until the pointer becomes a double-headed arrow.
2 Drag until the pane is the size you want.
3 Click in the outline pane to move to other slides for which you want to add notes.

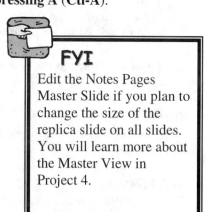

FYI

Edit the Notes Pages Master Slide if you plan to change the size of the replica slide on all slides. You will learn more about the Master View in Project 4.

Slide View

Use the slide view to display the slide pane in the most prominent position.

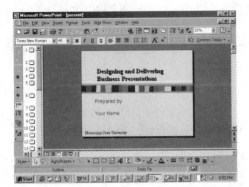

Outline View

Use the outline view to display the outline pane in the most prominent position.

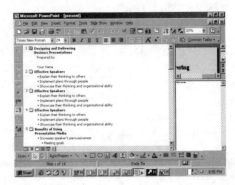

Switching to Slide View and Outline View

1   Click the Slide view button (on the status line at the bottom). Use the next/previous slide buttons or the token to move within the presentation in Slide view.

2   Click the Outline view button (on the status line at the bottom). Use the next/previous slide buttons or the token to move within the presentation in Outline view.

PowerPoint 97 users: Use the view buttons (on the status line) or click **View, Slide** to move to Slide view or **View, Outline** to move to Outline view.

Slide Sorter View

The Slide Sorter view displays every slide in a miniature format similar to the way one would sort 35mm slides on a light table. This view is convenient for adding, deleting, and moving slides, and adding slide transitions.

Switching to Slide Sorter View

1   Click the Slide Sorter view button (on the status line at the bottom) or click **View, Slide Sorter.**

2   Click **Zoom** (right side of the Standard Toolbar) and select 33 percent. You can now see all the slides on the screen without scrolling.

3   Set the Zoom on the setting of your choice (large enough that you can recognize the content of the slides but small enough to minimize scrolling to locate a specific slide).

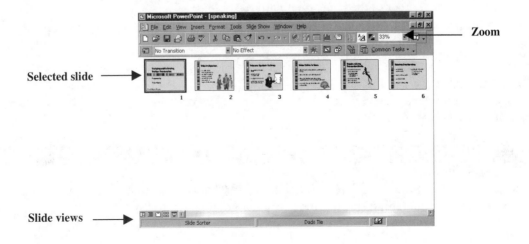

Zoom

Selected slide

Slide views

Deleting a Slide

1 Select the title slide by pointing to the slide and clicking. Note a bold border surrounds the selected slide as shown in the previous illustration.
2 Press **Delete**.
   Note: Click **Undo** (left arrow on the Standard Toolbar) to restore the deleted slide.

Deleting Multiple Slides

1 Select the title slide.
2 Hold down the **SHIFT** key and click another slide. Repeat to select additional slides of your choice.
3 Press **Delete**.
   Note: Click **Undo** (left arrow on the Standard Toolbar) to restore the deleted slides.

Duplicating a Slide

1 Click **Edit, Duplicate** (or Ctl-D). A duplicate of the selected slide appears as the next slide in the presentation.

Copying and Moving a Slide

1 Select the second slide.
2 Hold down Ctrl and drag the selected slide to the beginning of the slide show. Note an icon with a plus sign at the top appears as you drag the slide indicating an object is being moved.
3 Release the mouse button (drop) when a vertical line marker appears to left of Slide 1. This marker indicates a position where a slide can be dropped.
4 Delete the duplicate slide now positioned as Slide 1.

FYI

Make a duplicate of a slide when
— Creating a slide with similar design elements to ensure consistency and save time.
— Experimenting with a design enhancement. You can return to the original design without reformatting the slide. Simply delete the duplicate slide containing your trial format and resume formatting the original slide.

Resequencing Slides

1 Select the title slide.
2 Click and drag the selected slide to its new position (the end of the presentation) and release the mouse button (drop). A vertical line marker appears to indicate when you have reached a position where a slide can be dropped.
3 Repeat the procedure to return the title slide to its original position. Repeat to reinforce the resequencing procedure.

Slide Show View

This view is used to run a full-screen presentation for preview on your monitor or to project the slide show while a speaker is presenting.

Moving to Slide Show View

1 Move to Slide 1 in Normal or Slide Sorter view.
2 Click **View, Slide Show** or click the Slide Show view button. The first slide is displayed.
3 Press **Escape** to return to the presentation window.

Presenter's Tip

To deliver a presentation with professional style and high impact, you must remain in slide show view at all times — even when an audience member asks you to return to a previous slide. You'll learn to run your presentation like a polished professional in Project 2.

Learning Objectives

➢ Change the slide layout of an existing slide to ensure consistency and efficiency.
➢ Create a simple bulleted list and a bulleted list with multiple levels.
➢ Add clip art to a slide that does not contain a clip art placeholder.
➢ Search the Microsoft Clip Art Gallery and Microsoft Clip Art Live Web Site to locate relevant, engaging clip art.
➢ Add slide transitions and use custom animation effects to add impact and target the audience's attention.
➢ Print a presentation in various formats: slides, handouts, notes pages, and outline view.
➢ Run a presentation in a seamless manner during a presentation.

Choosing an Appropriate Slide Layout

You can change slide layouts after you have keyed text. Keep in mind that using an AutoLayout rather than fine tuning the slide manually will save you time and ensure consistency in the size and placement of design elements. To illustrate this principle, you will change the layout from a bulleted list to a bulleted list with clipart layout.

Changing the Slide Layout

Directions: Follow the instructions to revise Slide 2 (shown at right).

1 Be certain the presentation file **Speak** you created in Project 1 is open.

2 Display Slide 2 in Slide view.

3 Click **Slide Layout** icon (from Standard Toolbar or the Common Tasks Toolbar).

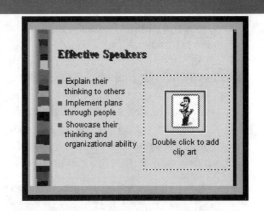

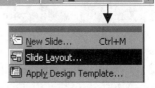

4 Select **Text and Clip Art** as the slide layout.
5 Click **Reapply**.
6 Continue developing this slide in the next section.

FYI

You could have inserted clip art on this slide without changing the layout by simply clicking **Insert, Clip Art (or clip art button on the Draw toolbar)**. The clipart would be inserted in the center of the slide (as shown at the right). Thus, you would need to resize the bulleted list placeholder and resize and reposition the clip art.

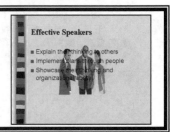

Adding Clip Art to a Slide

Including clip art on a slide can engage the audience's attention, reinforce an important point, and help the audience visualize a complex idea. Clip art can be selected easily from the Microsoft Gallery or Microsoft's web site. Once inserted, the clip art can be sized and positioned to achieve the desired effect.

Adding Clip Art in a Clip Art Placeholder

Directions: Follow the instructions to revise Slide 2 (shown at right).

1 Double-click the clip art placeholder on Slide 2. The photos section of the Microsoft Clip Art Gallery appears:

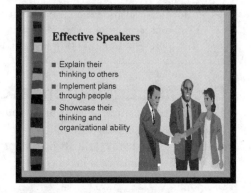

2 Click the category you desire and then the desired clip art image. Click **OK**.
3 Select the clip art (sizing handles appear). Point to a corner handle and hold down **Shift** as you drag outward to enlarge the clip art slightly.
4 Point to the center of the clip art and drag it down to the bottom right quadrant of the slide. This position provides a realistic perspective and avoids the impression that the people are floating on the page.

FYI

A link automatically takes you back to the Microsoft Gallery when you double click on a clip art image. Then select a different piece of clip art to replace your previous selection.

Using the Find Function to Locate Clip Art in the Clip Art Gallery

Directions: Follow the instructions to build Slide 3 (shown at right).

1 Create a new slide with the **Text & Clip Art** AutoLayout.
2 Key the slide title and the bulleted list.
3 Double-click on the clip art placeholder. The Microsoft Gallery appears.
4 Input a keyword in the keyword box (e.g., speaker). Press **Enter.** A gallery of clip art images matching the key word appears.

5 Click a clip art image of your choice that depicts an effective speaker and thus reinforces the main idea in the slide. Click **Insert**.

Designer's Pointer

Research shows that people notice graphics second only to headings. Optimum placement of a graphic (clip art or chart) supporting text is the lower right quadrant of the slide. Your graphic acts as a "draw" to pull the viewer's eye from the title area, through the text area, to focus on the graphic.

Inserting Clip Art Without a Clip Art Placeholder

Directions: Follow the instructions to revise Slide 4 (shown at right).

1   Create a new slide with the **Bulleted List** AutoLayout.
2   Key the slide title and the bulleted list (shown at right).

Insert Clip Art

3   Click **Insert, Picture, Clip Art** (or Clip Art button on the Draw toolbar).

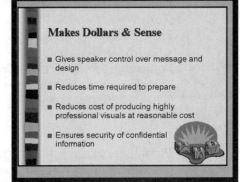

Makes Dollars & Sense

- Gives speaker control over message and design
- Reduces time required to prepare
- Reduces cost of producing highly professional visuals at reasonable cost
- Ensures security of confidential information

—— **Clip Art**

4   Continue developing this slide in the next section.

Importing Clip Art from Microsoft's Web Site

Directions: Follow instructions to download a clip art image from Microsoft's web site.

1   Click **Clips Online** from the menu bar at the top of the Microsoft Gallery dialog box.

—— **Clips Online**

FYI

You can import image files you have downloaded from the Internet or other sources. Just click **Import Clips** from the menu bar at the top of the Microsoft Gallery dialog box. Browse to locate the image file and insert.

2   Wait while your Internet browser opens and connects to Microsoft's web site.
3   Click a category from the tabs at the top of the screen (clip art, pictures, sounds, motion).
4   Input a keyword (e.g., money) into the search panel. You can also browse through the categories. A gallery of images matching the keyword appears.
5   Click the **red down arrow** below the image you want to download. A dialog box appears giving you the option to open or save the image to disk.
6   Click "Open it." The image should be displayed in the Microsoft Clip Gallery for easy insertion into presentations.
7   Move the clip art to the bottom right quadrant of the slide and size to fit.

Trouble Shooting Tip

If you receive an "unknown file type prompt when you attempt to download an image from Microsoft's web site (or other sites), click **Pick App**… and **OK**. Then the option to open or save will appear.

If you download the image to disk, you must decompress the file to insert it in the Microsoft Gallery. To decompress the file, go to Windows Explorer and double click the image file name.

Creating Bulleted Lists with Multiple-Levels

You will learn to promote and demote text in a bulleted list to show the relative importance of each item (e.g., major or minor point within an outline).

Promoting and Demoting Text in a Bulleted list

Directions: Follow the instructions to revise Slide 5 (shown at right).

1 Click **New Slide** and select the **Text & Clip Art** AutoLayout.
2 Key the slide title and the first major point ("Increases speaker's persuasiveness").
3 Press **Enter**.
4 Click the **Demote** button (right arrow on the Formatting toolbar or press **Tab**) to begin the second level or minor point of this bulleted item.

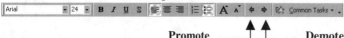

Promote ———↑ ↑——— Demote

5 Press Enter and key the second minor point.
6 Click **Promote** button (left arrow on the Formatting toolbar or press **Shift+Tab**) to move back the first level of bulleted items.
7 Complete the bulleted list.
8 Add relevant clip art.
   PowerPoint 97 users: Select this image from the "Screen Bean" category.

Trouble Shooting Tip

You may need to recolor the clipart to provide higher contrast between the clip art and the slide background. If your slide background is black, you may not be able to see the screen bean at all. You will learn to recolor clip art in Project 3.

Creating a Two-column Bulleted List

Directions: Follow the instructions to revise Slide 6 (shown at right).

1 Create a new slide with the **2 Column Text** AutoLayout.
2 Key the slide title and both columns of the bulleted list.
3 Click the left column bulleted list placeholder. Key the text.
4 Click the right column bulleted list placeholder. Key the text.

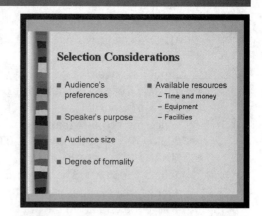

Designer's Pointer

Too much text and too many meaningless images clutter a visual. An audience will ignore an image perceived to be complicated or concentrate on deciphering the slide and not listen to the speaker. Keep your audience's attention by designing clean, uncluttered slides. To avoid clutter,
• Leave 60 to 70 percent of the slide blank.
• Follow the 7 x 7 rule: Limit text to 7 lines per slide and 7 words per line.

Adding Slide Transitions

Slide transitions add impact to the way one slide replaces another when you are running the presentation. Transition effects include blinds, box in, box out, cover, split, uncover, and wipe, etc. Guidelines for applying transitions effectively are provided in the presenter's tip on page 20.

Adding Transition Effects to Slides

1   Display your presentation in Slide Sorter view (click the Slide Sorter view button or **View, Slide Show**).

Note: The Slide Sorter toolbar is automatically displayed.

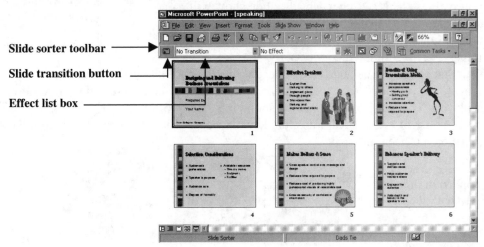

Slide sorter toolbar

Slide transition button

Effect list box

Add a Transition Effect for All Slides

2   Click the **Slide Transition** button on the Slide Sorter toolbar or click **Slide Show, Slide Transition**. The Transition Dialog box appears.

PowerPoint 97 users: To display the transition dialog box, you must use the menu commands; a button does not appear on the Slide Sorter toolbar.

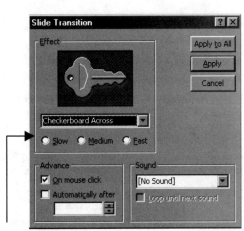

Set to advance slide

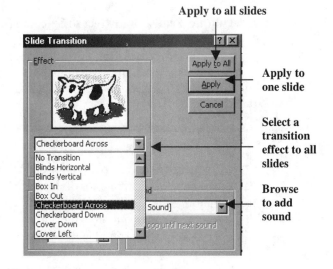

Apply to all slides

Apply to one slide

Select a transition effect to all slides

Browse to add sound

3 Click the down arrow to display the list of transition effects.

4 Select a transition effect of your choice.

5 Select the speed of the transition by clicking **Fast** (or slow or medium). A preview of the selected effect appears each time you click a speed setting. Note the image of a key is replaced with the image of a dog.

6 Become familiar with each of the transition effects. Then, select the **Wipe Right** effect at a **Fast** speed setting.

7 Note the default for advancing to the next slide is "on mouse click." This setting means the slide show will advance to the next slide when the speaker clicks the mouse. In Project 3, you will learn to set automatic timings between slides.

FYI

Display the Transition dialog box when you need to preview the effects, to add sound as the slide transitions in, and to add automatic timings. Otherwise, select a transition effect directly from the Slide Sorter toolbar.

8 Note that sound can be added to play each time the slide show advances. You simply click the arrow to the right of "No Sound" and browse to locate a sound file you wish to play as this slide is displayed. You will learn more about sound in a later project.

9 Click **Apply to All.** A small transition icon appears below the selected slide to indicate that a transition has been set.

Denotes effect applied to slide selected (Slide 1)

Icon denoting slide transition effect

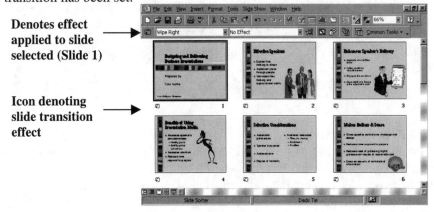

Add a Unique Transition Effect to Selected Slides

10 Select Slide 1 (the title slide).

11 Select the **No Transition** effect for this first slide directly from the Slide Sorter toolbar.

12 Click **Apply** to add this new transition effect to Slide 1 only.

Presenter's Tip

1. Create a systematic pattern for slide transitions. For example, choose two transition effects; one for the slides and one for divider slides — slides that you add to mark the beginning of each major section of your presentation. You might use a different transition for each section of a long presentation to give the audience a change of pace. You will not need a transition for the first slide when you plan to display your first slide prior to a formal introduction.

2. Create a blank slide with no transitions as the last slide; this nondistracting slide may remain on the screen during a question-and-answer period. Alternately, you can change your preferences to end a slide show with a black slide (**Tools, Options, View, End with Black Slide.**)

Enhancing with Custom Animation

Custom animation allows the speaker to add impact to a presentation and to direct the audience's attention to important points. Custom animation involves identifying objects the speaker wishes to display at his/her discretion rather than displaying all objects at the same time the slide is displayed. Additionally, a bulleted list may be displayed all at once or point by point with or without a dimming effect depending on the speaker's purpose. Creative effects can be produced by (a) introducing text a letter or word at a time rather than all at once and (b) adding relevant sound clips to selected objects.

Inserting Custom Animation

1   Display Slide 2 in Slide View.
2   Click **Slide Show, Custom Animation**. The Custom Animation dialog box appears. (Alternate: **Right click, Custom Animation**).

Select the Objects to Be Animated

3   Be sure the **Order & Timing tab** is selected.
4   Click in the box in front of "Text 2" and "Object 3" to indicate you wish to animate these two objects. "Text 2" and "Object 3" now appear in the Animation Order box.

Alter the Animation Order of Animated Objects

5   Click "Text 2" in the Animation Order box.
6   Click the down arrow and change the animation order of "Text2" (the bulleted list) to appear as the second animated object. "Object 3" (the clip art) will now appear first.
7   Click **Preview** and note the animation:

Title:	"Title 1" box is unchecked; thus, the title automatically appears when the slide is displayed.
Clip Art:	"Object 3 appears first in the Animation order box; thus, the clip art appears after the mouse is clicked once.
Bulleted List:	"Text 2 appears second in the Animation order box; thus, the bulleted list appears after another mouse click.

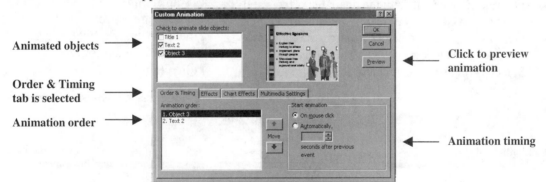

Animated objects ⟶

Order & Timing tab is selected ⟶

Animation order ⟶

⟵ Click to preview animation

⟵ Animation timing

Set the Timing of the Animated Object (Object 3, Clip Art)

8   Note the default is for the clip art to appear "on mouse click" — when the speaker advances the slide show with a mouse click (or other methods discussed in Project 1). In Project 3 you will learn creative techniques using automatic timings of objects.

Select an Effect for the Clip Art

9 Click the **Effects** tab.

10 Familiarize yourself with the available effects and directions for "entry animation and sound." Click the down arrows and select an effect and a direction. Then, click **Preview** to view your choices.
PowerPoint 97 users: Select from one drop-down menu that contains all possible combinations of effects and directions.

11 Select **Stretch** for the effect and **Across** for the direction.

Object 3 highlighted ────▶

Select an effect and direction ────▶

Browse to add a sound file ────▶

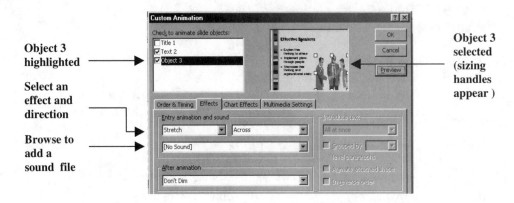

Object 3 selected (sizing handles appear)

Select a Sound for the Clip Art

12 Click the down arrow beside "No Sound." Browse to view the available sound files.

13 Select a subtle sound such as **chime**.

Select an Effect for the Bulleted List

14 Familiarize yourself with the available effects and directions for "entry animation and sound." Click the down arrows and select an effect and a direction. Then, click **Preview** to view your choices.

15 Select **Wipe** for the effect and **Right** for the direction.

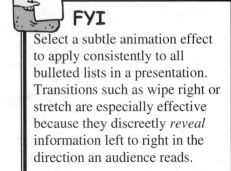

FYI

Select a subtle animation effect to apply consistently to all bulleted lists in a presentation. Transitions such as wipe right or stretch are especially effective because they discreetly *reveal* information left to right in the direction an audience reads.

Text 2 highlighted ────▶

Effect and direction ────▶

Dim effect ────▶

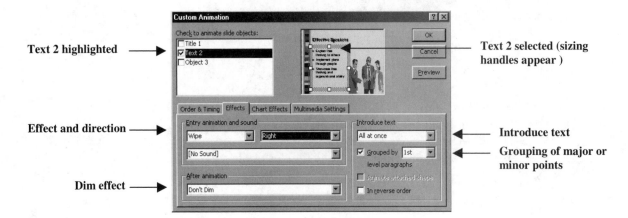

Text 2 selected (sizing handles appear)

Introduce text

Grouping of major or minor points

Select a Method of Introducing Text (Bulleted List)

16   Click the down arrow below "Introduce Text" and note the options for displaying the text in this bulleted list: all at once, by word, and by letter.

17   Retain the default value of introducing the text all at once.

18   Note the options for the amount of text that is displayed with one mouse click:

Ungrouped: A mouse click displays the entire bulleted list at once if the check mark is removed from before "grouped."

Grouped by 1st level: A mouse click displays a major point *and* all subpoints.

Grouped by 2nd level: A mouse click displays the main point only; a second mouse click is needed to display each subpoint.

19   Retain the default value of grouped by 1st level.

Adding a Dimming Effect to Previously Displayed Bulleted Items

20   Click the right arrow below "After Animation

."

21   Select a color for the dimming effect by clicking a color from the choices provided. To select from additional colors, click **More Colors** and select from the color choices displayed.

Note: When you advance to the next bulleted item, the previous item appear in the color you selected — preferably a slightly lighter color that can still be read easily by the audience.

22   Go to Slide Sorter view and note the build icons to the right of the transition icons on each of the slides that includes a build effect on a bulleted list.

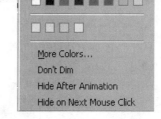

> ## Presenter's Tip
>
> When bulleted lists are animated, the slide is built one bulleted item at a time. Disclosing text progressively allows the speaker to control the flow the information for targeted impact. Bulleted lists that are discussed as a unit should not be built (e.g., a slide previewing major points in the presentation or subpoints within a major point). Building bulleted lists is comparable to moving a blank sheet of paper down an overhead transparency to uncover points as they are discussed.

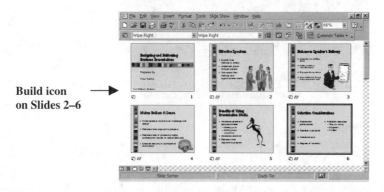

Build icon on Slides 2–6

Animate the Other Slides in the Presentation

  23   **Slide 1 — Designing and Delivering Business Presentations** (None)

   Slide 2 — Effective Speakers
   1st: Clip art — stretch across
   2nd: Bulleted list — wipe right

   Slide 3 — Enhances Speaker's Delivery
   1st: Clip art — stretch across
   2nd: Bulleted list — wipe right

   Slide 4 — Makes Dollars and Sense
   1st: Clip art — dissolve
   2nd: Bulleted list — wipe right

   Slide 5 — Helps Speakers Accomplish Goals
   1st: Clip art — peek from right
   2nd: Bulleted list — wipe right

   Slide 6 — Selection Considerations
   1st: Bulleted list (left) — wipe right
   2nd: Bulleted list (right) — wipe right

Printing a Presentation

PowerPoint allows you to print your presentation in several ways. The following section focuses on printing your presentation as slides, handouts, notes pages, and outline view. A later project will be devoted to creating highly professional handouts and notes pages.

Printing a Presentation

  1   Click **File, Print**. The Print dialog box appears.

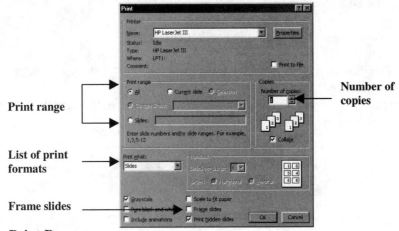

Print range

List of print formats

Frame slides

Number of copies

Choose the Print Range

  2   Note the three print ranges:

   To print all slides: Select **All**.

   To ***print a specific slide:*** Select **Current Slide**. (The slide displayed or the one selected in the Slide Sorter View will print.)

   To ***print multiple slides:*** Select Slides and input the number of slides in the dialog box to the right (e.g., 2,3,5-12).

  3   Click **All** in the Slide Range list box.

Select the Type of Printout

4 Click the down-arrow in the **Print What** list box and note the four types of output that can be produced.

Slides: Prints a full-screen view of the slide. Use this option to print slides directly on transparency acetates to be projected on an overhead projector.

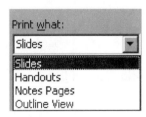

Handouts: Prints an audience handout of slides in various formats (e.g., number of slides per page in a vertical or a horizontal orientation).

Notes pages: Pages with miniature slide at the top and notes for uses described in Project 1 (See slide views).

5 Click **Handouts** and note the options for number of slides per page:

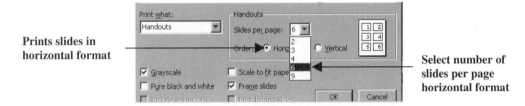

Prints slides in horizontal format

Select number of slides per page horizontal format

6 Click **6** slides per page.
7 *PowerPoint 2000 Users:* Note the order of the slides can be changed from the horizontal default value to vertical. Click Vertical and note the preview provided. Retain the default to print the slides horizontally across the page.

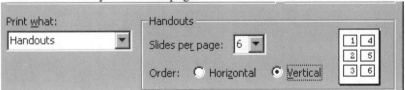

8 Click **Frame Slides** to add an attractive border around each slide.
9 Click **OK**.
10 Refer to the previous instructions and produce the following printouts:
— Audience handouts of Slides 1–3 printed three slides to a page in vertical order.
— All slides in outline view.
— Full-screen of Slide 1, 3, 4 to be used to create acetate transparencies.
— Notes page of Slide 2.

Delivering a Presentation

Learning to run your slide show professionally is essential to ensure a successful presentation. You will learn efficient, foolproof ways of moving around in your slide show that will keep the audience's attention focused on the speaker—not the technology. A presenter's tip provides additional advice for delivering a seamless presentation.

Moving Within a Presentation

1 Display Slide 1 in Slide view.
2 Click the Slide Show button. The slide show starts running in full-screen view beginning with Slide 1, the slide that was active when you began the show.
3 Complete the following instructions to learn to run your presentation professionally. Try the mouse and the keyboard methods to determine the method most convenient for you.

Advance to the next slide

4 *Mouse:*   Left mouse click
   Keyboard: Enter, space bar, right arrow key, or page down

Return to the previous slide

5 *Mouse:*   Right mouse click
   Keyboard: Left arrow key or page up

Move to a specific slide

Keyboard Method

6 Input the slide number using the numerals on the alphanumeric keypad.
7 Press **Enter**.

Mouse Method

8 Right click the mouse button. Perform the following functions from the drop-down menu:
   a.   Select **Next** to move the next slide.
   b.   Select **Previous** to move back one slide.
   c.   Select **Go**, **Slide Navigator**, and select a slide from the list provided.

   d.   Select **Go**, **By Title,** and select a slide from the list provided.

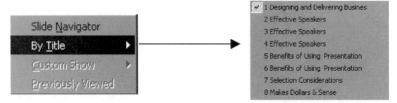

9 Practice moving around your slide show inputting specific numbers and using the right mouse click.

End a slide show

10   Press **Escape** to exit the slide show view. You will return to the Slide view of Slide 1, the active slide when you clicked the Slide Show button.

Presenter's Tip

To appear polished and professional, keep the slide show in Slide Show view at all times. Your audience should see the full screen view and not the untidy work areas (e.g., slide sorter, slide, or outline views). Practice the mouse and keyboard controls to avoid any klutzy moves that will diminish your professional delivery.

Additional Techniques to Ensure Professional Delivery

1 Display Slide 1 in Slide view and then click the Slide Show button to begin running the presentation.

Black out the screen

2 Press the **B** key on the keyboard. The screen becomes black.
3 Press the **B** key again to return to the slide.

White out the screen

4 Press the **W** key on the keyboard. The screen becomes white.
5 Press the **W** key again to return to the slide.

End the Presentation with a Black Screen

6 Click **Tools, Options, View**.
7 Click **End with Black Slide**.
8 Run your slide show again and note the black slide that appears at the end. Advance once more to exit the slide show.

End with black slide →

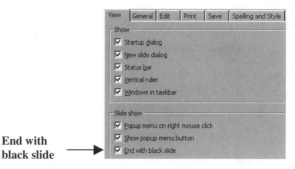

Presenter's Tip

Practice these techniques to make your delivery appear virtually invisible and effortlessly executed:

* Set PowerPoint to end the presentation with a black slide so you do not have to be concerned about advancing past the last slide and exiting to one of the other views.
* Use the right arrow key or page down to move to the previous slide. Avoid the urge to right click with the mouse because this command displays a drop-down menu that requires you to locate the slide from the slide navigator. This procedure is time consuming and directs the attention to the technology and away from the speaker.
* Number the slides on your speaker's notes so you can quickly display a slide needed to answer an audience member's question. There is no need to exit to the slide sorter view to locate the correct slide or right click and display the slide navigator. Just input the specific slide number and move effortlessly back to a previously displayed slide or advance forward to new slides if you believe the question warrants reordering the sequence of your presentation.
* Use the black and white out technique when an audience member asks a question just as you advance to a new slide. Removing the new information will keep your audience focused on your answer to the question and will allow you to transition into the new topic as you had planned.

Project 3
Using Drawing Tools, Clip Art, WordArt, Photographs, and Sound to Enhance a Presentation

Learning Objectives
➢ Create drawn objects to enhance slides.
➢ Ungroup and rotate clip art.
➢ Use WordArt to add dramatic effects to text.
➢ Insert photographs as a slide object and a slide background.
➢ Add sound to slide objects and slide transitions.

Using Drawing Tools to Enhance a Presentation

You will learn to enhance the basic presentation you created in Projects 1 and 2 with drawn objects, clip art, WordArt, photographs, and sound. First, you will add drawn objects, such as rectangles and ovals, to add a creative flair to a slide or to enhance the appearance of a piece of simple clip art. You will explore various way of enhancing the drawn objects with color, lines, shadows, and other effects.

Enhancing A Title Slide
Directions: Follow the instructions to enhance the original slide as shown.

Original Slide

Enhanced Slide

1 Open the file **Speak** and display Slide 1 in Slide view.

Remove the Background Graphic Object
2 Click **Format, Background**.
3 Click to remove the check in front of "Omit Background Graphics from Master."
4 Click **Apply** to remove the object from the title slide only.

Add Relevant Clip Art
5 Select a clip art image that depicts a successful business presentation and insert (**Insert, Picture, Clip Art** or click the **Clip Art** button on the Draw toolbar).
6 Size and position the clip art as shown on the model. Note the clip art is large because you are creating the setting for a presentation. Refer to the Designer's Pointer.

Designer's Pointer
Anchor the clipart at the bottom of the slide and make it large enough to create the impression that the audience is involved in this setting rather than simply "plastered" on the slide.

Create a Projection Screen to Showcase the Slide Title

7 Click the rectangle icon on the Draw toolbar. Drag to draw a rectangle that will create the appearance of a projection screen behind the speaker.

Rectangle tool ⌐   ⌐ Clip art

8 Resize and position to create the desired perspective.
9 Format the rectangle (referred to as an *AutoShape* in PowerPoint) using the icons on the Draw toolbar:
   a. Click the list arrow to the right **Fill Color**. Select an off white color similar to the color of an actual projection screen.
   b. Click the list arrow to the right of **Pen Color**. Select a color slightly lighter than the background color.
   c. Click **Shadow**.
      — Select the first shadow effect (shadow appears at the top left of the object).

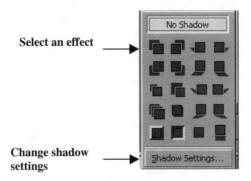

Select an effect →

Change shadow settings →

      — Click **Shadow** again and click **Shadow Settings**. The Shadow Settings toolbar appears.

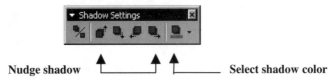

Nudge shadow   Select shadow color

      — Click the right arrow next to **Shadow Color** to select the color of the shadow.
      — Click the up arrow key two times to enlarge the size of the upward shadow slightly.

10 Move the text box containing the title so that it appears to be projected in the center of the projection screen.
11 Highlight the title and select a creative font face (e.g., Comic Sans) and font size of at least **40 points** to create a dramatic effect.

Reformat Presenter's Identification

12 Key your name (the presenter) above your company/university name in the placeholder at the bottom left of the screen. Resize and position.
13 Format the text box containing the presenter's name and affiliation:
   a. Click the Border Fill button on the Draw toolbar and select one of the complimentary colors provided on the colors dialog box.
   b. Click the Shadow button on the Draw toolbar and select a shadow color slightly lighter than the border fill color.

14   Format the text (presenter's name and affiliation):
    a.   Choose an interesting font face and font size of at least **18** points.
    b.   Select a font color that contrasts well with the border fill color.

Delete the Sub-Title
15   Select the original placeholder for the sub-title.
16   Click **Delete**.

Trouble Shooting Tip

If you are having trouble deleting a placeholder, it is likely not selected. See if the cut and copy icons are active or ghosted (not active). If you clicked the placeholder once, you will have a diagonal border between the sizing handles, and the cut and copy icons will be ghosted — a sign you cannot delete or copy this placeholder. Point to the diagonal border and click again. The border will become shaded and the cut and copy icons will be active. The placeholder is selected, and you can delete the placeholder.

Apply a Patterned Background for Higher Impact
17   Click **Format**, **Background**.
18   Click the list arrow to the right of the color bar.

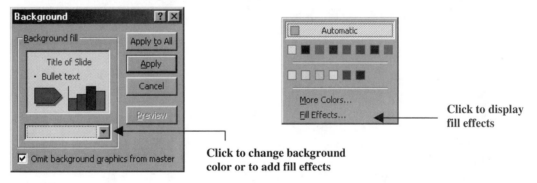

Click to change background color or to add fill effects

Click to display fill effects

19   Click **Patterned**.
20   Select a pattern from the gallery that appears in the Fill Effects dialog box.
21   Select a foreground and a background color that are complimentary with your template colors.

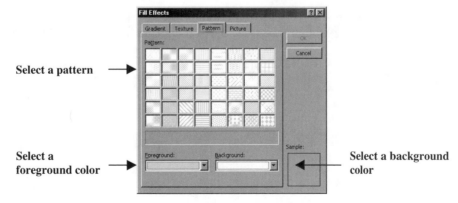

Select a pattern →

Select a foreground color →

Select a background color

22   Click **Apply**.

Using an Autoshape to Enhance Clip Art

Directions: Follow the instructions to enhance the original slide as shown

Original Slide

Enhanced Slide

1 Display Slide 5 in Slide view.

Create a Stage for the Screen Bean

2 Click **AutoShapes**, **Oval** and draw the stage below the screen bean.

Oval tool

Change the Order of the Objects (Clip Art and Stage)

3 Click to select the AutoShape (stage). Sizing handles appear around the stage.
4 Click **Draw, Order, Send to Back** to send the stage behind the screen bean.
5 Size and position the AutoShape and the screen bean to create the desired effect.

Format the Shape

6 Add a textured fill:
   a. Click the list arrow beside **Fill Color** on the Draw toolbar.
   b. Click **Fill Effects**, **Texture**.
   c. Select a texture that resembles a floor (brick, hardwood) from the gallery that appears in the Fill
      Effects dialog box.

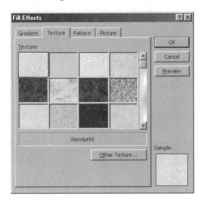

Designer's Pointer
To position objects precisely, select the object, then use the arrow keys to move the object up, down, left, or right a short distance.

7 Make other format changes to achieve a desired effect: pen color, line style, dash style, shadow, or 3D.

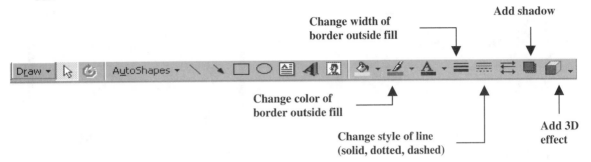

Group the AutoShape and Another Object

8 Click the AutoShape (the stage) to select it. Sizing handles will appear.

9 Point to the screen bean and hold down the Shift key as you click (**Shift + click**). Sizing handles now appear on the screen bean and the AutoShape (as shown in the illustration).

10 Click **Draw, Group**.

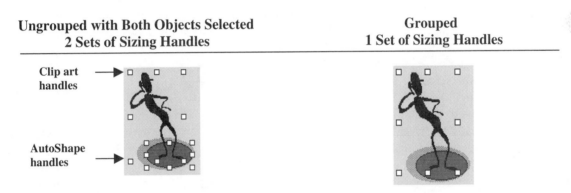

Ungrouped with Both Objects Selected
2 Sets of Sizing Handles

Grouped
1 Set of Sizing Handles

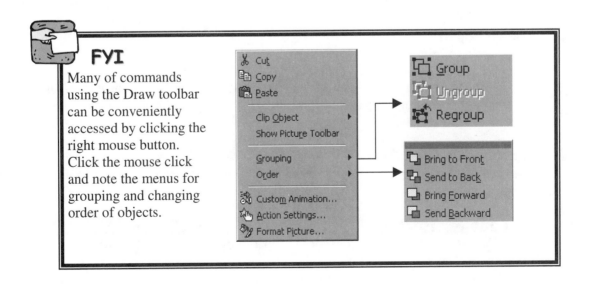

FYI

Many of commands using the Draw toolbar can be conveniently accessed by clicking the right mouse button. Click the mouse click and note the menus for grouping and changing order of objects.

Adding an AutoShape to Enhance a Bulleted List Slide

Directions: Follow the instructions to enhance the original slide as shown.

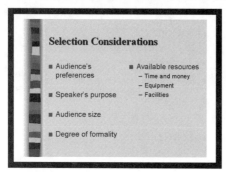

Original Slide

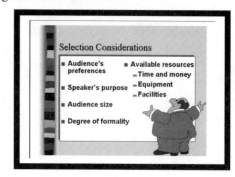

Enhanced Slide

1   Display Slide 6 in Slide view.

Create a Projection Screen Behind the Bulleted List
2   Select the **rectangle** AutoShape on the Draw toolbar and draw the projection screen.
3   Resize and position to create the impression of a projection screen behind the two-column list.
4   Send the AutoShape behind the bulleted lists (Click **Draw, Order, Send to Back** or use the right click).
5   Format the AutoShape to create the effect of a projection screen:
   a. Change the fill color to an off white color.
   b. Select a pen color and line style.
   c. Add a shadow and adjust the shadow color and width of shadow. Refer to the instructions for enhancing the title slide with a shadowed rectangle at the beginning of this project if necessary.
   d. Add other creative effects of your choice.

> **Designer's Pointer**
> This slide illustrates how changing the order of objects gives the ability to creative dramatic effects to an otherwise bland, dull slide. Note the effect created by placing the clip art in front of other objects on the slide.

Add Relevant Clip Art
6   Insert clip art to create the impression of a speaker delivering a presentation.
7   Change the order of the clip art so that the speaker is standing in front of the projection screen.
8   Size and position the clip art to achieve proper balance and perspective.

Working with Clip Art
You can increase the usefulness and appeal of clipart by applying the following techniques: recoloring, ungrouping, rotating, and cropping.

Recoloring Clip Art
Directions: Follow the instructions to recolor the clipart in Slide 5.
1   Display Slide 5 in Slide view.
2   Select the screen bean. The Picture toolbar should appear. If it does not, click **View, Toolbars, Picture** to display it.
3   Select the list arrow in the "After" column and select a new color.

4   Click **Preview** to see the change.

5   Click **OK** when you have made all the necessary changes.

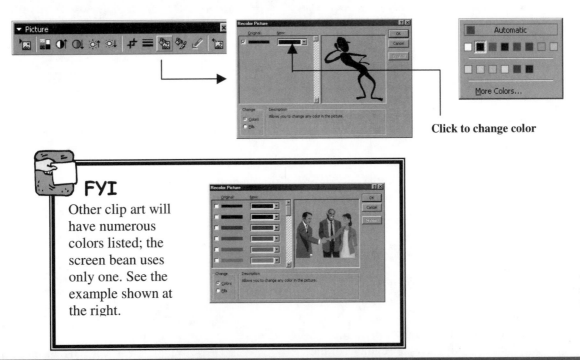

Click to change color

FYI

Other clip art will have numerous colors listed; the screen bean uses only one. See the example shown at the right.

Ungrouping Clip Art

The slide at the left illustrates three common errors in slide design: (1) a bulleted list must have at least two bullets, (2) clip art is too small and thus looks lost and out of place on the slide, and (3) uninteresting design does not accomplish the speaker's goal. The slide should dramatically unveil the speaker's startling statistic regarding the average business presentation to reinforce the major point that improvements in speaking skills are needed.

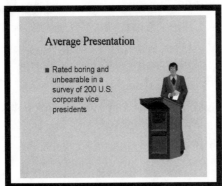

Ineffective Slide

Enhanced Slide

Directions: Follow the instructions to enhance the original slide as shown.

1   Go to the Slide Sorter view and click to the right of the last slide in the presentation (Slide 6, Selection Considerations).

2   Create a new slide using the **Title Only** AutoLayout.

3   Insert clip art of an unenthusiastic speaker delivering a presentation.

4   Resize and position the speaker as shown in the model.

Create a Dialog Box for the Audience's Comment

5 Click **AutoShapes, Callouts** on the Draw toolbar. Select one of the four balloons in the top row.

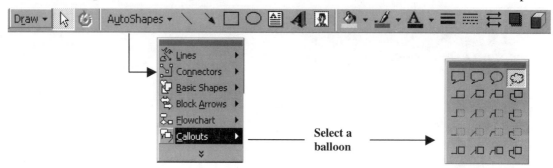

Select a balloon

6 Key the following text in the callout box: **Boring and unbearable**.

7 Format the callout box as desired (border fill, pen color, line style, shadow, 3D).

8 Format the text as desired (font face, font size, and font color, print attributes such as bold, shadow, etc.).

Create the audience

9 Insert the clip art shown at the right from the "People at Work" category.

10 Ungroup the clip art:

   a. Click **Draw, Ungroup**. Sizing handles now appear for each the segment of the ungrouped clip art.

   b. Click outside the clip art to deselect all sections of the image.

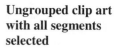

Ungrouped clip art with all segments selected

11 a. Delete the whiteboard:

   — Point at the whiteboard to select it. Sizing handles appear around the whiteboard.

   — Press **Delete**.

   b. Delete the teacher.

   — Point at the teacher to select it. Sizing handles appear around the teacher.

   — Press **Delete**.

Handles for whiteboard

Handles for teacher

12 Regroup the audience:

   a. Select the remaining segments of the clipart:

   — Click the first segment and **Shift + Click** on all other segments.

   b. Click **Draw, Group** (or **right click**).

Trouble Shooting Tip

Selecting all segments of a clip art image that has many small segments is difficult. An easy trick is to left click and drag as you draw a box to surround the entire clip art. When you release the mouse, the sizing handles will appear. Should you have missed a segment, hold down the Shift key as you point to the unselected segment. Of course, you could click outside the clip art image to deselect the entire image and then redraw the box.

Add the source note

13   Create a new placeholder and key the text for the source note: **200 U.S. corporate vice presidents surveyed**.

14   Resize the text box to display the text on two lines.

15   Position the source note beneath the speaker.

16   Fine tune the size and position of each object (speaker, audience, callout box, and source note) to produce a realistic effect.

Designer's Pointer

Text in source notes should be at least 14 points for a typical presentation room. This size is large enough for the audience to see. The source provides credibility to the slide but should not assume a prominent point of emphasis on the slide.

Add Custom Animation and Sound

17   Click **Slide Show, Custom Animation.** Refer to Project 2 to review custom animation if necessary.

18   Edit the Custom Animation dialog box to create the following effects:

a.   Click the **Order & Timing** tab. Select the objects to be animated and set the animation order:
Unanimated: Slide title, speaker, and audience (will come in with the slide).
1st: Callout box
2nd: Source note. automatically **.2** seconds after the callout box appears.

b.   Click the Effects tab and select effects.
— Callout box — dissolve effect (or effect of your choice).
— Source note — appear.

c.   Set an automatic timing on the source note so that it will come in automatically **.2** seconds after the callout box appears (previous event). No mouse click is necessary to bring this object in.
— Click **Order &** Timing tab.
— Click **Automatically** in the Start Animation box.
— Input **.2** seconds after previous event in the spin box.

Two objects animated

Select Order & Timing tab

Set automatic timing

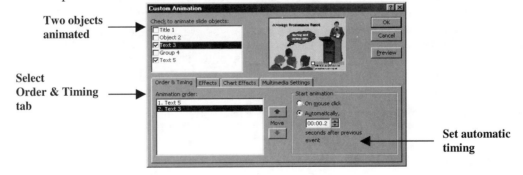

Note: You will learn more about advanced animation techniques in Project 5.

Add a Sound Effect

19   Click **Slide Show, Custom Animation**.

20   Click the **Effects** tab and click the callout box in the animation box at the top.

21   Click the right arrow next to **Sound** to display available sound clips and select one.

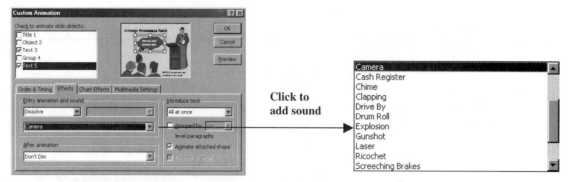

Click to add sound

22 If you have an Internet connection, complete this activity:
   a. Study the techniques for locating sound file on the Internet or commercial software programs in the FYI feature box and the Designer's Pointer on page 39.
   b. Locate a yawn or bored sound file and download to your hard drive or a floppy disk.
   c. Click the list arrow next to **Sound** again. Scroll to the bottom of the list and click **Other Sound**.
   d. Browse to locate the downloaded sound file.
   e. Press **OK**.

FYI

An abundance of clip art, photographs, video clips, and sound files is available to help a speaker illustrate key concepts or points. Regular commercial software or public domain or shareware clip art galleries are available. You can also download multimedia files from the Internet.

The licensing agreement of *commercial clip art* allows the user to use the art on one computer at a time and as part of any document or publication you choose to distribute (same stipulation as with other commercial software). You may not share clip art via a network without a site license. *Public-domain software* is not copyrighted and is free to the public except for a small fee to cover the cost of disks. When using images downloaded from the Internet, read the copyright agreement carefully to avoid copyright infringement.

Rotating Clip Art

AutoShapes can be rotated easily by simply clicking on the rotate tool on the Draw toolbar and then dragging the object in the desired direction. A clip art image cannot be rotated until it is converted to an object. Converting a clip art image to an object breaks the link to the Microsoft Clip Art Gallery. Thus, double clicking on the object will not advance directly to the Microsoft Clip Art Gallery. The following activity illustrates additional editing power you gain from converting a clip art image to an object.

Directions: Follow the instructions to complete Slide 8 (shown at right). You may substitute other clip art images if these images are not available on your system.

1 Go to the Slide Sorter view and click to the right of the last slide in the presentation (Slide 7, Average Presentation Rated).
2 Create a new slide using the **Title Only** AutoLayout
3 Key the title in the title placeholder.
4 Insert the clip art image of the duck and the computer.

5   Select the image and click **Draw, Ungroup** and delete the computer and table.

6   Repeat the ungroup command and delete the duck. Ungroup again to delete the shadow below the hammer. Only the hammer should remain.

7   Insert the image of the angry man and size and position as shown on the model.

8   Select the hammer and move it on top of the man's hand.

9   With the hammer selected, click the **Free Rotate** tool located on the Draw toolbar.

Free rotate tool

Note the sizing handles become green circles after you click the rotate tool.

10   Point to one of the green circles and drag until you reach the desired angle.

Note: If you need to rotate an object left or right or flip it horizontal or vertical, click **Draw, Rotate or Flip,** and the desired direction. For example, use the rotate left or right if need your clip art image to face in the opposite direction.

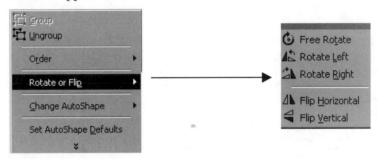

11   Send the hammer behind the man's hand by clicking **Draw, Order, Send to Back**.

12   Continue this slide in the next section.

Designer's Pointer

You can also download images and sound from the Internet. Several web sites are suggested for helping you locate "the perfect" images for your presentations.

Images: Lycos.com, Hotbot.com, video.com, and webplaces.com
Sound: WavCentral.com and webplaces.com

You are encouraged to look for other sites and to share the addresses with your class and instructor.

Inserting WordArt

1 Click the **WordArt** button on the Draw toolbar.

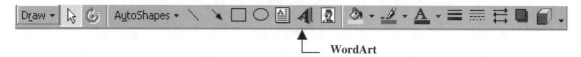

WordArt

2 Choose a design from the Word Art Gallery. The Edit WordArt Text dialog box appears.

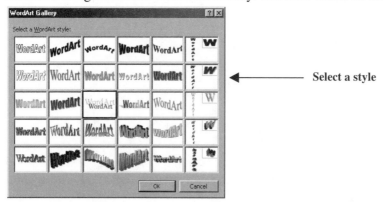

Select a style

3 Make these changes in the Edit WordArt dialog box:

   a. Input the text: **Keep your cool!**

   b. Select a font face and font size.

Select a font face and size

Key text

4 Note a WordArt toolbar appears on the Draw toolbar after you input text in the WordArt dialog box.

Return to Gallery

Change shape

Changes to vertical text

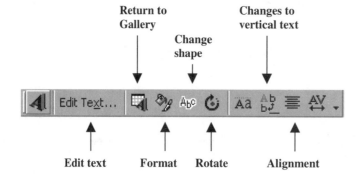

Edit text   Format   Rotate   Alignment

5 Click the **Format WordArt** button and select a fill color and a border color complimentary with your background.

6   Click the **ABC** button and select a shape for the WordArt (e.g., can up).

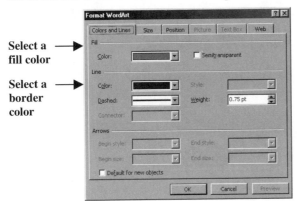

Select a
fill color →

Select a
border
color →

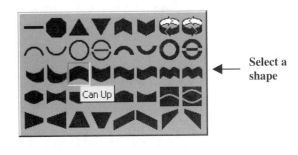

← Select a
shape

7   If necessary, click the **Rotate** button. Point to a green circle (replaces the sizing handles) and drag until the WordArt is slanted exactly the way you wish.

8   Animate the slide:
   Unanimated: Title and clip art (come in with the slide).
   1st: WordArt — an effect of your choice.

Creating Screen Captures

Directions: Follow the instructions to complete Slide 9 (shown at right).

1   Create a new slide to appear after Slide 8 (Handling Hecklers). Use the **2-column Text** AutoLayout.

2   Key the title and bulleted lists.

3   Display the Page setup dialog box: Click **File, Page Setup**

4   Edit the Page Setup menu to appear exactly as you wish it captured:
   a.   Select **Overheads** in the "Slides sized for."
   b.   Click **Portrait** in the "Slides orientation" section.

5   Hold down the **Alt key** as you press **PrintScreen** (key located to the right of the F12 key).
   Note: The paste icon becomes active denoting you have copied an object to the clipboard.

6   Press **Escape** to return to your slide.

7   Click in the area on the slide where the screen capture will appear.

8   Click **Paste**.

9   Continue building this slide in the next section.

Cropping Images

1   Select the screen capture. The Picture toolbar should appear when the image is selected. If not, click **View, Toolbars, Picture**.

2   Click the cropping tool on the Picture toolbar.

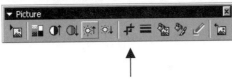

Select cropping tool

3   Point to the sizing handle in the right center of the selected object. Drag to the left to crop the image to the right of the arrow in the illustration.

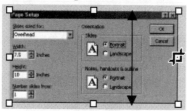

4   Create a text box and key the commands: Click, **File, Page Setup**.
5   Center the textbox directly above the screen capture. Format the font face and font size.
6   Use the rectangle tool on the Draw toolbar to create a showcase box to surround the text box and the screen capture.
7   Select the rectangle and send it behind the screen capture and the text box (**Draw, Order, Send to Back**).
8   Create an appealing format for the showcase box:
    a.   Click the **Fill Color** on the Draw toolbar and click **No Fill**.
    b.   Select an attractive pen color and line style from the Draw toolbar.
9   Group the showcase box, text box, and screen capture so the group can be animated to enter at once.
10   Animate the slides:
    Unanimated: Title (come in with the slide).
    1st: Bulleted list — wipe right with a build effect (grouped by 1st level)
    2nd: Grouped image — zoom in from screen center

Using Photographs to Enhance a Presentation

Photographs are used to help the audience visualize actual persons, places, or objects. Photographs can be added as a slide object or as the slide background.

Inserting a Photograph as a Slide Object

Directions: Follow the instructions to complete Slide 10 (shown at right). Your photo will vary.
1   Create a new slide to appear after Slide 9 (Converting Slides to Overheads). Use the **Title Only** AutoLayout.

Select a Photo
2   Select a photo using one of the following methods:
    a.   Click the **Clip Art** button on the Draw toolbar to open the Microsoft Gallery and download a photo from Online clips (from the Microsoft Clip Art Live Gallery).
    b.   Download a file from an Internet site or digital camera.
    c.   Scan a photograph.

If possible, select a photo that fits the tone of the presentation **Speak**, effective speaking development.
Refer to the Designer's Pointer on page 39 for a handy list of Internet sites containing multimedia objects.

3   Key a title in the title placeholder that fits the photo you selected.

Add a Creative Border for the Photograph

4   Click **Line Style** on the Draw toolbar.

L **Line style**

5   Click **More Lines**. The Format Picture dialog box appears.
6   Select a line color that is complimentary with other template colors.
7   Input **14 points** for the line weight. Click **OK**.

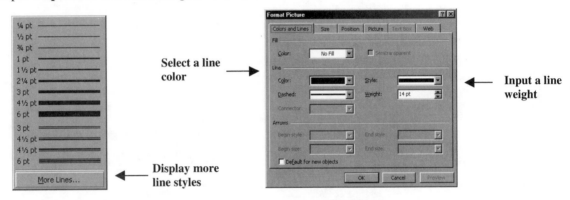

Select a line color →

Input a line weight ←

Display more line styles ←

8   Click the **Shadow** button on the Draw toolbar and add a shadow of your choice. Edit the shadow settings to select a light shade of the pen color.
9   Animate the slide:
   Unanimated: Title (come in with slide).
   1st: Photograph — dissolve effect

FYI

Generic photographs from Microsoft or other commercial galleries are available but may be inappropriate for a specific presentation. You can use a scanner to scan photographs taken with a regular camera and convert the photograph to an image that can be imported into your presentation. You can use a digital camera to capture the photograph as a computer file that can be imported into a presentation without developing the film.

Inserting a Photograph as the Slide Background

Directions: Follow the instructions to complete Slide 11 (shown at right). Your photo will vary.

1   Create a new slide to appear as the last slide in the presentation. Use the **Blank** AutoLayout.

Select a Photo

2   Select the photo you wish to use. You may download a file from an Internet site or digital camera or a scanned image. Refer to the Designer's Pointer on page 39 for a handy list of Internet sites containing multimedia objects.

Insert the Photo

3   Click **Format, Background**.
4   Click "Omit background graphics from master" and click **Apply** to remove the template object from this slide only.
5   Click **Fill Effects, Picture, Select Picture**.
6   Browse to locate the photo file.
7   Click **OK**.

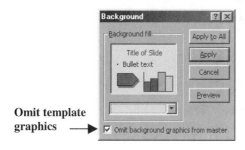

Omit template graphics

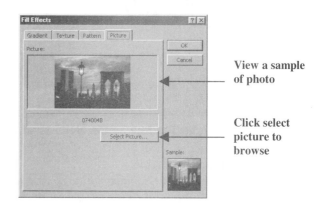

View a sample of photo

Click select picture to browse

Add a Slide Transition

8   Click **Slide Show, Slide Transition**.
9   Select **Dissolve** as the slide transition effect at **Fast** speed.
10 Add **Applause** as a sound effect.

FYI

This slide can be considered a "specimen slide" because it has a completely different format from the other slides in this presentation. Therefore, a new slide transition (different from the wipe right used on the other slides) can be used to add to the dramatic effect of this slide.

Designer's Pointer

Microsoft Photo Editor, the image editing software that comes with the Office 2000 or Office 97 suite, offers several tools for enhancing a photograph scanned or downloaded from a digital camera. Begin by opening your photograph file in Microsoft Editor and then experiment as you explore the menu options.

Effects. The first group of effects enables you to make minor adjustments to correct imperfections in the photograph. The second group of effects is used to add an artistic filter effect. Select a filter and then adjust controls for intensity, direction, etc.

Touch up and special effects →

Sharpen...
Soften...
Negative...
Despeckle...
Posterize...
Edge...

Artistic effects →

Chalk and Charcoal...
Emboss...
Graphic Pen...
Notepaper...
Watercolor...
Stained Glass...
Stamp...
Texturizer...

Image. Click **AutoBalance** to adjust the brightness and contrast levels of an image automatically or **Balance** to adjust manually. Use options on the crop menu to create attractive mats and oval and rectangular shaped images. Rotate images as desired using the options from the Rotate menu.

Crop...
Resize...
Rotate...

Balance...
AutoBalance

Only a few simple adjustments were made to improve the quality and to add an artistic flair to the original photograph shown at the right.

1. Apply the despeckle special effect to reduce a grainy look.
2. Apply the emboss special effect to add a creative texture and dimension.
3. Created the rounded edges:
   a. Click **Crop** and select rounded corners and specify the desired width. The space occupied by the rounded edges becomes white and must be made transparent

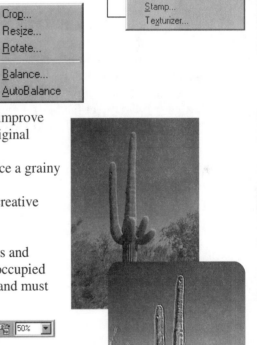

Set transparent color ↑

   b. Position the tool over the color you want to make transparent (the white edge), and click.
   c. A dialog box appears that shows the color that will change to transparent (white in this photo).
   d. Click **OK**.

Click white area where corners have been cut ↓

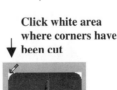

Inserting a Slide Transition

Directions: Follow the instructions to add slide transitions to the slides created in this project.

1 Display the presentation in Slide Sorter view.
2 Select any slides that do not include a slide transition icon below the slide.
3 Click the **Slide Transition** button on the Slide Sorter toolbar.
4 Select **Wipe Right** effect at a **Fast** speed setting.
   Note: This slide transition effect has been used for all other slides in this presentation except for Slide 11 (photograph as the background). This specimen slide requires a more dramatic effect.
5 Click **Apply**.

Print the Presentation

Directions: Print a copy of the file **Speak** as an audience handout with six slides per page. The slide should contain the following slides in order. Your instructor may instruct you to print the slides created or revised in Project 3 only (highlighted slides).

1 **Enhanced Title Slide**
2 Effective Speakers
3 **Average Presentation Rated**
4 Enhances Speaker's Delivery
5 **Helps Speaker Accomplish Goals (revised recolor clip art and stage)**
6 Makes Dollars and Sense
7 **Selection Considerations (revised with showcase box)**
8 **Handling Hecklers**
9 **Converting Slides to Overheads**
10 **Photo as Slide Object (slide title and photos will vary)**
11 **Photo Background (photo will vary)**

Project 4
Designing a Custom Template

Learning Objectives
➢ Edit the master slide to modify design elements in a PowerPoint presentation template.
➢ Modify a PowerPoint presentation template to fit the needs of a specific topic and audience.
➢ Creating a custom template to fit the needs of a specific topic and audience and to convey originality.

Customizing PowerPoint
Customizing PowerPoint allows the designer to adjust the design elements of a slide show to fit the needs of a particular topic and audience. Changes include (1) editing the slide master, (b) modifying an existing presentation design, and (c) designing a custom presentation design. Additionally, PowerPoint slides can be easily formatted to produce professional overhead transparencies.

Editing the Master Slide
The Slide Master controls the elements displayed in each slide. As a result, any revision that you input on the slide master automatically changes each slide in the presentation. Modifying the master slide rather than revising each slide individually increases your efficiency and ensures consistency in all slide elements.

Directions: Follow these instructions to modify the slide master in the file Speak. You will select a different font, modify and font size and color, and modify the font size and bullet selection for the first and second levels.

1 Be sure the file **Speak** is open.
2 Click **View, Master Slide**, **Slide Master**.

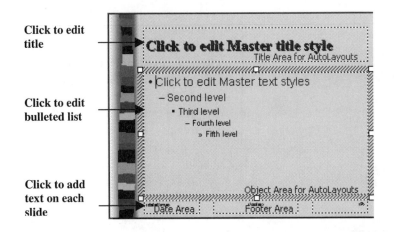

Click to edit title

Click to edit bulleted list

Click to add text on each slide

Trouble Shooting Tip
Changes that have been input on individual slides will not update to reflect modifications made on the Slide Master. Thus, avoid the temptation to modify slides as you build. Instead make all changes in design elements on the Slide Master.

Revise the Title Placeholder
3 Click in the placeholder titled **Click to edit Master title style**.
4 Select a sturdy font that can be read easily from a distance (e.g., Arial). Add bold and a shadow effect. Refer to the Designer's Pointer related to font selection.
5 Change the alignment to left align or center depending on your template's current setting.
6 Enhance the placeholder with a subtle but creative look. Select from these suggestions or develop ideas of your own:
   a. Change the color of the placeholder to a shade slightly darker than the slide background or a pattern to pull the placeholder forward slightly.
   b. Add a narrow border around the placeholder in a subtle color complimentary with the template.

Designer's Pointer

Choose sturdy font faces that can be easily read from a distance for projected visuals. Avoid (a) delicate fonts with narrow strokes that wash out especially when displayed in color, and (b) italic and decorative fonts and condensed fonts (letters are close together) that are difficult to read.

Good Choices	Poor Choices
Arial Black	*Times New Roman, Italic*
Times New Roman, Bold	**Impact**
CG Times	*Abadi MT Condensed*

Choose a strong font for the slide title to draw the audience's attention naturally to this idea first, and a less prominent but readable font for the text.

Modify a Bullet

7   Click in front of the words **Click to edit Master text styles** to modify the first-level bullet.

8   Change the font face and font size for the first level to a selection of your choice.

9   Click **Format, Bullet**.

10   Be sure the **Bulleted** tab is selected.
PowerPoint 97 users: You can only choose numbers; therefore, this dialog box does not appear. Skip to Step 11.
Note: Select the **Numbered** tab to select a numbering style in the bulleted list.

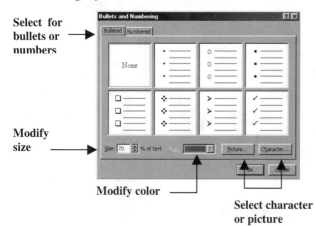

Select for bullets or numbers →

Modify size →

Modify color ⎯

Select character or picture

Designer's Pointer

Use fonts large enough for the audience to read and use font size to create a hierarchy of importance between the design elements (slide title, bulleted lists and source notes). The following ranges are general guidelines but should be adapted to fit a specific presentation setting. For example, slightly larger font sizes are required when presenting in large rooms and transmitting over compressed video during a video-conference.

Headings —24 to 36 points
Other text — 18 to 24 points
No text under 14 because it is not visible from a distance.

Note: You can change color and size in the Bullets and Numbering dialog box. If you are modifying the bullet, proceed to the next step and change the color and size in the next dialog box.

11   Click **Character** from the Bullet dialog box to select a character.
Note: You can select **Picture** to add a picture bullet. Experiment as time permits.

12   Select a new character:
a.   Click the **Bullets** drop-down list arrow and note the various categories of characters.
b.   Select the **Monotype Sorts** category and note the display of available characters.
c.   Click a character to select it.

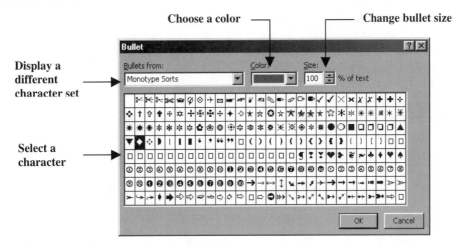

13   Increase the bullet size:
Double click in the **Size** text box and input a number larger than 100 percent.

14   Select a new color:
Click the **Color** list arrow and select a color from the selection of colors complimentary with the template.

15   Click **OK** after selecting a bullet and changing the size and color.

16   Click in the front of **Second Level** and repeat these steps to modify the appearance of the second-level bulleted items if time permits.

FYI

Letters are measured from the top of the highest extender to the bottom of the lowest extender. A letter measuring one inch is 72 points.

72pts.= 1 inch

48pts.   36pts.   24pts.   14pts.

Preview the Changes and Print Selected Slides

17   Exit the Slide Master by going to Slide Sorter view.
18   Note the modifications input on the Slide Master are reflected on each slide in the file.
19   Save the file using the file name **Speakrev**.
20   Print Slides 1–3 only as an audience handout 3 slides per page.

Modifying the Color Scheme of a Presentation Design

Changes in the Master Slide allow designers to customize the objects on slides to fit a particular presentation. Recall the modifications you made to fonts and bullets in the previous activity. Additionally, simple changes to the color scheme of a presentation design help a speaker convey a particular mood, to associate a presentation with a company or concept, or to give an original look to a familiar PowerPoint presentation. Refer to the Designer's Pointer for information related to color selection.

Directions: You will modify the presentation design you selected for the file **Speakrev**.
1 Open the file **Speakrev**.

Selecting a Standard Presentation Design
2 Click **Format, Slide Color Scheme**.
3 Be sure the **Standard** tab is selected.
4 Study the preview samples of the available standard color schemes. Colors are illustrated for design elements (background, title text, text, fills, and shadows).
5 Select one of the standard color schemes for the presentation design you selected for this presentation.
6 Click **Apply to All** to convert all slides in the file to the new color scheme.

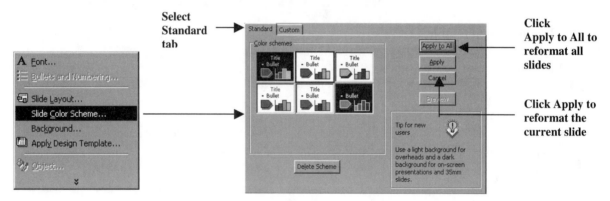

7 Evaluate the appeal of the new color scheme. Return to the standard color scheme to select another color (**Format, Color Scheme, Standard**) until you are satisfied with your choice.

Modifying a Standard Presentation Design
8 Click **Format, Color Scheme**.
9 Click the Standard tab and select the standard design that is closest to the design you prefer.
10 Click the **Custom** tab. Note the color choices for each design element in the presentation design (listed at the left of the Color Scheme dialog box).

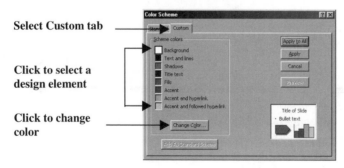

Selecting a Standard Color for the Background

11 Click **Background, Change Color**.

12 Be sure the Standard tab is selected.

13 Select a color for the slide background from the standard color wheel. Note the illustration shown at the right.

14 Click **OK**.

15 Evaluate the appeal of the new background color. Return to the custom color scheme to select another color (**Format, Color Scheme, Custom**) if necessary.

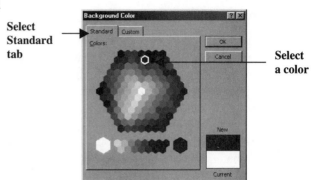

Select Standard tab

Select a color

Selecting a Custom Color for the Background

You can mix a custom color if the color you prefer is not on the standard color wheel.

16 Click **Background, Change Color**.

17 Select the **Custom** tab.

18 Select the exact color by clicking up and down the right color bar. Note the new color appears above the original color for easy comparison.

19 Evaluate the appeal of the custom color. Return to the background color dialog box and select another color if necessary.

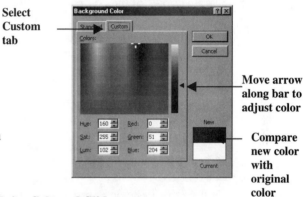

Select Custom tab

Move arrow along bar to adjust color

Compare new color with original color

Change the Color of Other Design Elements and Print Selected Slides

20 Make changes in the color of other design elements required because of the change in the background color. Refer the Designer's Pointer related to color choice.

21 Print Slides 1–3 only as an audience handout 3 slides per page.

Designer's Pointer

Several important factors affect your choice of an effective color in a presentation:

Formality and Effect: Conservative colors (blue) add formality; brighter colors (yellow) lend a less formal and perhaps trendy look. Also, blues and greens create a more relaxed and receptive environment than warm colors such as red, orange, or yellow.

Association: An audience naturally associates colors with certain ideas; e.g., green for money or go; yellow for caution; red for stop, danger, or financial loss; school colors, and company and product colors. Because of the natural association of red with financial loss, never use red in a table of numbers or a graph depicting growth or a healthy financial condition.

Differentiation: Color helps the audience distinguish between different design elements. For example, create a hierarchy indicating level of importance by selecting one color for the slide title and a different, less prominent color for the text (e.g., yellow for title and white for text on a blue background).

Output Media: and Contrast: Choose a color scheme that will be legible with the output medium you are using for your presentation; that is, the method you will use for producing your visuals — overheads, slides, or 35 mm slides.

- Dark-to-medium backgrounds with light foregrounds work best in a dark room (slides or projected slide show).
- Light backgrounds with dark foregrounds work best in a well-lit room (color transparencies).

Designing a Custom Presentation Design

A speaker representing companies in competitive business presentations must develop a strong custom presentation design (template) that clearly reflects a company's professional image and unique corporate identify. Use of stock presentation designs that provide no association with a company give the impression that a speaker is unprepared, pays little attention to details, and perhaps leads to the logical conclusion that the company this speaker represents is incompetent as well.

Directions: Follow instructions to create a custom template for a company of your choice or one designated by your instructor.

Research the Company and Prepare a Sketch

1   Obtain copies of the company's printed materials (letterhead, brochures, annual report) and visit the company's web site. Identify graphical elements, approved company colors and logos the company is already using to create the company's identify.
2   Review the Designer's Pointers in this project to be sure you understand design principles related to font and color selection.
3   Sketch a draft of your design.
4   Reproduce or download from the company's web site high quality images for use in the design. Keep in mind that poor reproductions will reflect negatively on the company.

Designer's Pointer

Follow this systematic process when selecting the color scheme of a custom presentation:

Choose the background color first because this area is the largest amount of color. Consider the issues affecting color discussed in a previous Designer's Pointer: formality, mood, association, differentiation, and output media.

Choose foreground colors — a color for the slide title and a second color for the text — with high contrast with the background for easy readability. Black text against a white background has the greatest contrast. A blue background with yellow text contrast well, but white text would be difficult to read because of the low contrast.

Evaluate the readability of the fonts with the color scheme you have selected. Colored text tends to wash out when projected; therefore, be certain the fonts are sturdy enough and large enough to be read easily.

Choose accent colors that complement the color scheme. Accent colors are used in small doses to draw attention to key elements; e.g., bullet markers, bars, fills, specimen text.

Project your presentation ahead of time in the room where you are to present so you can adjust the color scheme. This process is necessary because colors display differently on a computer monitor than a projection device. You can also double check the readability of the text in the actual room and proofread for errors.

Develop the Custom Design

5   Click **Blank Presentation** from the PowerPoint Startup Menu.
6   Create the first slide using the **Title** AutoLayout. The design contains no color or graphics.

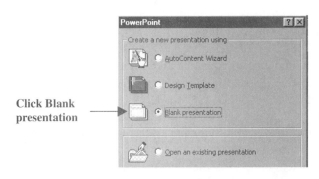

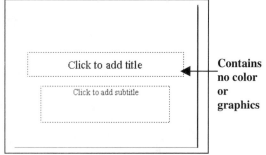

Click Blank presentation

Contains no color or graphics

7   Select the color scheme for each design element in the presentation (background, title, text, and accents). (Click **Format**, **Slide Color Scheme**.)

Designer's Pointer

In addition to choosing a readable font (sturdy font and large enough size), follow these guidelines for selecting an effective fonts for your custom template:

1. Choose an interesting font fact that conveys the mood of a presentation and is different from the fonts most commonly used (e.g., Times New Roman and Helvetica).

Formal, Conservative Presentation	Less Formal Presentation
CG Times	**Comic Sans MS**
Arial	Tahoma

2. Limit the number of fonts within a single presentation to no more than three to prevent a cluttered and confusing look.

3. Choose a serif and a sans serif font types to create a hierarchy of importance between the slide title and text as described:

Font Type	Description	Recommended Use
Serif	A serif font has short cross-strokes that project from the top and bottom of the main stroke of a letter — the type that typically read as the main print in textbooks and news-papers. *Example:* **CG Times**	Text
Sans serif	Has no cross-strokes (serifs). *Sans* means without. Has simple, blocky look that is appropriate for displaying text, as in the slide title or headlines of a newspaper. Example: **Arial**	Slide title

8   Edit the Master Slide

a. Select appropriate fonts to convey the intended mood.

b. Enhance placeholders with color, patterns, borders, shadowing (optional).

c. Add object(s) to the slide that communicate(s) your intended message. Animate this object if you wish. Suggestions include

— A logo or clip art image to represent your company or topic.

— A text box containing a short phrase that will keep the audience focused on the purpose of the presentation throughout the delivery (perhaps positioned in the bottom right corner).

— A series of borders or drawings that create a dynamic custom background.

d. Adjust the position of the placeholders in relation the objects. For example, if an object is covering the left one third of the screen (similar to Dad's tie), make the following adjustments:

— Select the title **and** the bulleted list placeholder.

— Drag until the placeholders are center over the right two-thirds of the screen leaving equal side margins.

Note: Selecting both placeholders will enable you to size and position the two placeholders precisely the same.

Create Slides

9   Create the title page and one bulleted list providing text of your choice (e.g., list the company's major products, locations, or significant achievements).

Print Slide Show

10   Print the slide show as an audience handout 3 slides per page.

Converting Slides to Overheads

PowerPoint Professional can be used to create professional overhead transparencies. When you know in advance your output medium is overheads, choose the blank presentation from PowerPoint's startup menu; select dark print (black or other dark colors). If you learn you must deliver the presentation using overhead transparencies after you have developed slides, a number of modifications are required. Modifications are driven by the requirements of the overhead projector and the time and expense involved in color printing. Additionally, consider reducing the number of slides because it will take more time to display overheads than to project slides.

Directions: Follow instructions to convert the presentation **Speakrev** to overhead transparencies.

1   Be sure the file **Speakrev** is open.

2   Resave the file using the file name **Overhead**.

Change the Slide Orientation to Portrait

3   Click **File, Page Setup**.

4   Click the list box for Slides sized for and click **Overheads**.

Note: The default is On-Screen shows.

5   Click **Portrait** for the orientation.

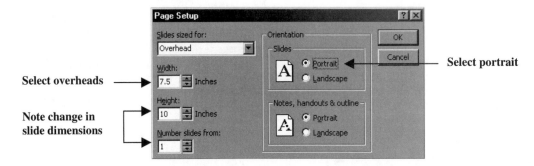

Modify the Color Scheme

6   Change the background to white.

7   Change the slide title and the bulleted list text a dark color.

Edit the Master Slide

8   Develop a design to create a hierarchy of importance between the slide title and text. Because you are limited to dark text, differentiate between the two levels with other creative techniques: vary font sizes, try adding bold and shadowing effects, a bright border around the title placeholder with an appealing fill effect, and creative ideas of your own.

9   Modify the objects on the slide to remove large areas of color and large logos that would require an inordinate amount of color. Your goal is to include "splashes of color" that clearly reflects the tone of the presentation.

Critique and Edit Slides

10   Redesign slides with animated layers (e.g., overlapping objects that hide after animation). Create a separate overhead for each layer or develop a simple bulleted list with appealing enhancements that require small amounts of color.

11   Check each slide for changes needed in the size and position objects because of the reduced width.

Save the Slide Show

12   Save the file as **Speakovd**.

Print the Slide Show

13   Print the slide show as an audience handout 3 slides per page.

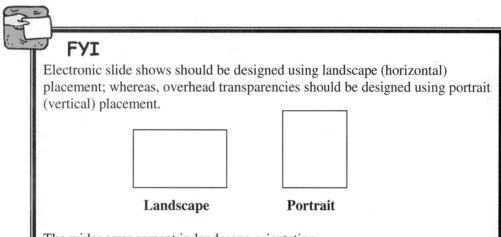

FYI

Electronic slide shows should be designed using landscape (horizontal) placement; whereas, overhead transparencies should be designed using portrait (vertical) placement.

Landscape   **Portrait**

The wider arrangement in landscape orientation

• Is more pleasing to the eye much like the soothing feeling of looking at a wide horizon.

• Makes longer lines available for bulleted lists and pictures.

• Is designed to fit the typical size of the projection equipment. The bottom of a vertically arranged slide (portrait orientation) would be cut off.

Learning Objectives

➢ Use automated timings to enhance a slide and to allow the presenter to deliver a slide show in a seamless manner.
➢ Create dazzling effects with hide after mouse click and hide after animation techniques.

Creative Animation Techniques

Animation directs the audience's eyes to a specific object as you have already seen in the simple animation used in Project 2 (e.g., building a bulleted list and bringing in objects in a specified order). Learning the three advanced animation techniques presented in this project will empower you to create effects that will reinforce important points in ways that will dazzle your audience. These techniques include (1) using automated timings, (2) using hide after mouse click animation, and (3) using hide after animation.

Note: You may revise the file **Speak** or **Speakrev** when completing Projects 5-10 depending on your preference of a background.

Using Automated Timings

Directions: Follow the instructions to enhance the original slide as shown.

Original Slide

Enhanced Slide

1 Create a new slide to appear after Slide 2 (Effective Speaker). Use the **Title** Only AutoLayout.
2 Click the **Clip Art** button on the Draw toolbar and insert the puzzle from the "Shapes" category shown in the model.
3 Resize the clip art so that it fills the slide leaving adequate margins on all four sides. Refer to the model for an example.

Ungroup the Clip Art

4 Select the clip art. Click **Draw, Group, Ungroup** (or right click, **Grouping, Ungroup**).
5 Click **Yes** at the prompt to convert to an object. A set of sizing handles will appear for each arrow.

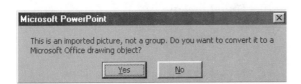

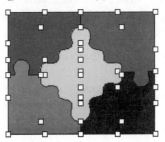

6   Click outside the clip art to deselect all parts of the
image.

Create a Text Box Inside the Puzzle Piece
7   Create a text box and key the text:
Commitment to the topic.
8   Format the text in the text box:
a.   Select an appealing font with a font size large
enough for the audience to read.
b.   Balance the text attractively on two lines if
necessary.
c.   Position the text box so that it is centered in the
top left puzzle piece.

Trouble Shooting Tip

Be careful not to move any of the
ungrouped pieces. Otherwise, the puzzle
will not fit together correctly when the
pieces are brought together during
animation. Use the **Undo** button to return
the piece to its original location if you
accidentally move a piece.

Create the Remaining Pieces Using the Copy Feature to Ensure Consistency
9   Select the completed text box and hold down **Ctrl** as you drag the text
box. An icon with a plus sign appears as you drag the slide indicating
an object is being moved.
10   Drop the text box and position in the center of another puzzle piece.
11   Repeat the process until you have created all the boxes.
12   Edit the text in each copied text box to create the following boxes:

Top left: Commitment to the topic (already keyed)
Top right: Solid organization and content
Bottom left: Compelling visuals
Bottom right: Strong delivery skills
Center: Winning presentation (placed in the most compelling position)

Group the Puzzle and the Related Text Box
13   Click the puzzle piece.
14   Hold down **Shift** and click the text box.
15   Click **Draw, Group** (or right click and click **Grouping, Group**).
16   Repeat to group the remaining puzzle pieces and text boxes.

Animate the Puzzle Pieces
17   Click **Slide Show, Custom Animation**
18   Be sure the **Order & Timing** tab is selected.
19   Click to select each of the five puzzle groups to be animated. These objects will appear in the
Animation Order box.
20   Set the animation order as follows:
1st   Commitment to topic
2nd   Solid organization and content
3rd   Compelling visuals
4th   Strong delivery skills
5th   Winning presentation

Designer's Pointer
If a title (slide or chart title or labels) is
longer than one line, arrange it in the
inverted pyramid format; that is, make
each succeeding line shorter than the
line preceding it.

Unbalanced:
Ten Common Mistakes Made
by Presenters

Inverted Pyramid Format:
Ten Common Mistakes
Made by Presenters

Set Automated Timings and Animation Effects

Automated timings will allow the speaker to focus on the audience while the puzzle pieces come in automatically one after the other — no mouse click is needed.

21   Be sure the **Order & Timing** tab is selected.

22   Select the first puzzle piece (Commitment to topic).

23   Click **Automatically** in the Start Animation box.

24   Input **.1 seconds** after previous event in the spin box.

25   Repeat for the remaining pieces.

Set Animation Effects

26   Click the **Effects** tab.

27   Click **Effects** and select the following effects for each object:

Commitment to topic	Fly from top left
Solid organization and content	Fly from top right
Compelling visuals	Fly from bottom left
Strong delivery skills	Fly from bottom right
Winning presentation	Dissolve, spiral, or swivel (a more dramatic effect than other groups)

Using the Hide after Mouse Click Animation Technique

Directions: Follow the instructions to enhance the original slide as shown.

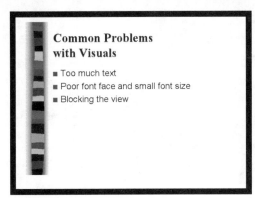

Original Slide

Enhanced Slide

1   Create a new slide to appear after Slide 6 (Selection Considerations). Use the **Title Only** AutoLayout.

2   Key the title in the title placeholder.

Create Layer 1

3   Use the AutoShapes rectangle to create a projection screen that serves as a backdrop or showcase box for your illustrations of the common problems with visuals.

4   Select a fill color and border color, line width and style, and any shadowing effect to give the projection screen a realistic appearance. Refer to the instructions for creating the showcase box to enhance the title slide (created in Project 3) if necessary.

Layer 1

5 **Create a text box:**
   a. Key the text: **Too Much Text**. Select an appealing sans serif font face (e.g., Univers or Arial) and set the font size at **40 points**.
   b. Key the words for the body of the visual. Select an appealing serif font (e.g., Times New Roman) as the font face and set the font size at **34 points**.

6 Center the text box in the projection screen as if it were being projected.

7 **Animate Layer 1:**
   a. Click **Slide Show, Custom Animation**.
   b. Set the animation order and effects as follows:
      1st: Rectangle — appear effect
      2nd: Text box — fly from the left or an effect of your choice.

8 Set the after animation effect so that the text box (Too Much Text) will hide after you click the mouse to move to the next object:
   a. Be sure the **Timings & Order** tab is selected.
   b. Click the list arrow beside After Animation.
   c. Select **Hide After Mouse Click**.

9 Check your animation selections with the dialog box provided.

Trouble Shooting Tip

You cannot use the Preview to verify the hide after animation for a first layer. A slide advances forward when the last object has been displayed regardless of the entry in the after animation box. After you have created the second layer, click **Preview** or go directly to slide show to check the animation.

Animate title and text box ➤

Select an effect and a direction ➤

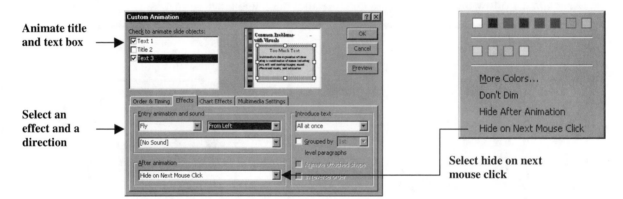

Select hide on next mouse click

Create Layer 2

10 **Create the text box for Layer 2:**
   a. Make a copy of the text box for Layer 1:
      — Select the text box you created for the first layer.
      — Hold down the Ctrl key as you drag the object over into the gray area outside the slide.
   b. Edit the title to read: **Poor Font Selection**.
   c. Edit the body:
      — Delete the dense text.
      — Click the **Bullets** icon on the Formatting toolbar and key the five bullets.
      Note: The bulleted points are as follows: **text, still images, sound effects and music, animation, and video.**
      — Select a narrow, hard-to-read font face and set the size at no larger than **18 points.**
      Refer to the Trouble Shooting Tip on page 61 if you need help formatting the bulleted list.

11 Drag the second text box and position it directly over the text box for Layer 1.

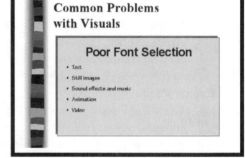

Layer 2

Trouble Shooting Tip

To adjust the space between the bullet and the text, the horizontal ruler must be displayed. Click **View, Ruler** and click **Ruler**. The horizontal ruler appears above your slide when the slide is displayed in Slide view or Normal view. To adjust the spacing, select the bulleted list placeholder and drag the indent marker to the desired location. All bulleted items at that level change to the new position.

Drag the indent marker to new indent setting.

12   Animate the text box in Layer 2:
   a.   Click Slide **Show, Custom Animation**.
   b.   Click to animate the text box. Select the same animation effect and direction you set for the text box in Layer 1.
13   Set the after animation effect so the text box (Poor Font Selection) will hide after you click the mouse to move to the next object:
   a.   Be sure the **Timings & Order** tab is selected.
   b.   Click the down arrow beside After Animation.
   c.   Select **Hide on Mouse Click**.
14   Click **Preview** and check the results:
   a.   The title appears with the slide.
   b.   A mouse click brings in the projection screen.
   c.   A mouse click brings in the first text box (Too Much Text).
   d.   A mouse click hides the first text box (leaves the rectangle blank) and brings in the second text box (Poor Font Selection).

Trouble Shooting Tip

To simplify working with layers, set the Zoom at 25 percent so you will have a large desktop area to the right of the slide. Drag all layers except the bottom layer off the slide into this work area. Start with Layer 1 on the slide. After you have positioned and edited the custom animation for Layer 1, drag Layer 2 on top of Layer 1. Continue with Layer 3 and so on.

Additionally, you may find it helpful to move Layers 1 and 3 to the desktop so you can view the objects in Layer 3 (text box and clip art) in front of the projection screen as you size and position them. Once the items are grouped, move them back to the work area until you are ready to add Layer 2 to the final slide.

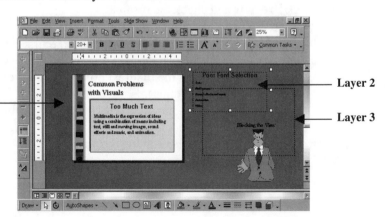

Layer 1 on the Slide and Layers 2 and 3 on the Desktop

Create Layer 3

15 Create the text box for Layer 3:

a. Select the text box you created for the second layer.

b. Hold down the Ctrl key as you drag the object over into the gray area outside the slide.

c. Edit the title to read: **Blocking the View.**

d. Delete the bulleted list.

16 Drag the third text box and position it directly over the title of the text box for Layer 2.

17 Insert a clip art image of a speaker facing forward directly in front of the projection screen.

18 Group the text box (Blocking the View) and the clip art so the group can be animated to appear at once.

19 Animate the group in Layer 3:

a. Click **Slide Show, Custom Animation**.

b. Click to animate the group. Select an animation effect of your choice (e.g., peek from right).

20 Set the after animation effect. The text box in Layer 3 does not require the hide after mouse click because the next mouse click advances to the next slide.

a. Be sure the **Timings & Order** tab is selected.

b. Click the down arrow beside After Animation.

c. Select **Don't Dim**.

Layer 3

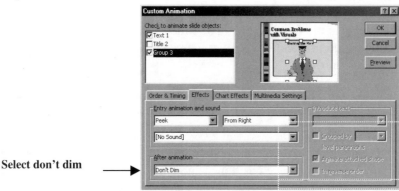

Select don't dim

21 Click **Preview** and check the results.

a. The title appears with the slide.

b. A mouse click brings in the projection screen.

c. A mouse click brings in the first text box (Too Much Text).

d. A mouse click hides the first text box (leaves the rectangle blank) and brings in the second text box (Poor Font Selection).

e. A mouse click hides the second text box (leaves the rectangle blank) and brings in the grouped object (Blocking the View).

f. A mouse click advances to the next slide.

Using the Hide After Animation Technique

Directions: Follow the instructions to enhance the original slide as shown.

1 Create a new slide to appear before the photo background slide. Use the **Title Only** AutoLayout. (Refer to the list of slides on the next page if necessary.)
2 Key the title in the title placeholder.
3 Insert a clip art image of an effective speaker. Size and position as shown in the model.

Create the Stars
4 Click **AutoShapes**, **Stars and Banners**.
5 Select the **5-point Star** and draw the star.

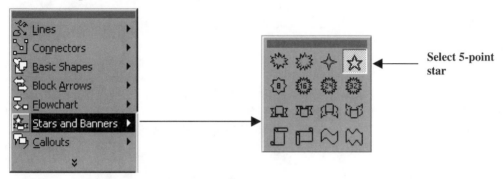

Select 5-point star

Create a Master Star
6 Select the star and click the **Rotate** button on the Draw Toolbar and drag to create a more realistic twinkling effect.

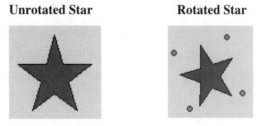

Unrotated Star   Rotated Star

7 Size the star and position directly over the word *Star* in the slide title.
8 Send the star behind the title placeholder (**Draw, Order, Send to Back**).
9 Animate:
   a. Click **Slide Show, Custom Animation**.
   b. Set the animation order and effect:
       Unanimated: Title and clip art
       1st: Star 1 — dissolve. Set after animation color to dim to white.
   c. Set the automated timing:
       — Be sure the **Order and Timing** tab is selected.
       — Select a star and click **Automatically** in the Start Animation box.
       — Input **0 seconds** after previous event in the spin box.

Copy the Master Star to Create Additional Stars

10 Select the star and hold down **Ctrl** as you drag the object. An icon with a plus sign appears as you drag the slide indicating an object is being moved.

11 Drop the star anywhere on the screen; you will reposition later.

12 Repeat the process until you have created several stars (refer to the model to view a possible placement of stars).

13 Be creative as you reposition the stars in various places on the slides and vary the size to create an appealing design.

Slide in Slide Show View After Animation Has Been Executed

Animate the Stars

The slide at the right that illustrates the appearance of the slide after the animation has run. Compare this actual slide display with the slide as it would be appear in the Slide view (model on previous page). Note some stars remain after the animation; other stars dissolve in and disappear. Use your own creativity to choose the arrangement of the animated objects that will remain and those that will hide.

14 Click **Slide Show, Custom Animation**.

15 Set the animation order of each star.

16 Select slides to be hidden after animation:

    a. Identify each star that you wish to hide after animation.

    b. Edit the custom animation by clicking **Hide After Animation** in the After Animation list box.

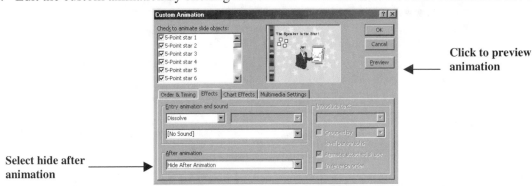

Click to preview animation

Select hide after animation

17 Preview the animation and edit until you have achieved a dazzling design.

Add a Slide Transition

18 Click the **Slide Transition** button on the Slide Sorter toolbar.

19 Select a dazzling slide transition for this slide (e.g., split vertical out or dissolve). Like the photograph as a background, this slide can be considered a specimen — one of a kind.

Printing the Presentation

Directions: Print a copy of the file **Speak** as an audience handout with six slides per page. The slide should contain the following slides in order. Your instructor may instruct you to print the slides created in Project 5 only (highlighted slides).

1	Enhanced Title Slide	8	Selection Considerations
2	Effective Speakers	9	**Common Problems with Visuals**
3	Average Presentation Rated	10	Handling Hecklers
4	**Keys to Effective Speaking**	11	Converting Slides to Overheads
5	Enhances Speaker's Delivery	12	Photo as Slide Object (slide title & photos will vary)
6	Helps Speaker Accomplish Goals	13	**The Speaker Is the Star**
7	Makes Dollars and Sense	14	Photo Background (photo will vary)

Learning Objectives

➢ Design an effective table.
➢ Design an effective bar chart and pie chart.
➢ Change the chart type after building a chart.

Creating Tables

Displaying text in columnar format aids the speaker in clarifying large quantities of data. PowerPoint simplifies the process of creating highly professional tables.

Creating a Table

Directions: Follow the instructions to enhance the original slide as shown.

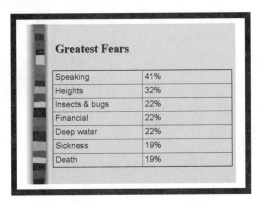

Ineffective Slide   **Enhanced Slide**

1 Create a new slide to appear after Slide 1. Use the **Table** AutoLayout.
2 Key the title in the title placeholder.
3 Double click in the table placeholder.
4 Enter **2** for number of columns and **7** for number of rows.
5 Key the data for the table.

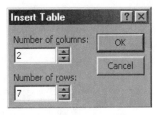

Resize and Reposition the Table

6 Highlight the second column. Point the right border, when the two-headed arrow appears, drag to the left to reduce the space between the columns.
7 Select the table and position the table in the center of the slide.

Format the Data

8 Highlight the second column and click Right Align from the Formatting toolbar.
9 Highlight the first row (Speaking) and boldface for added emphasis.

Format the Table

10 Be sure the table is selected. Right click and click **Borders and Fills**.
11 Click the **Borders** tab. Select a line style, color, and width.

12 Click the buttons until a border surrounds only the outside of the table (Refer to the model to view the border.)

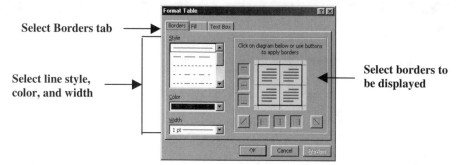

Select Borders tab ⟶

Select line style, color, and width ⟶

Select borders to be displayed ⟵

13 **Add a Fill Behind Table:**
   a. Click the **Fill** tab.
   b. Click the list arrow beside color and select a fill color complimentary with the template colors.

14 **Add Shading Behind the First Row:**
   a. Highlight the first row (Speaking).
   b. Right click and click **Borders and Fill** and the **Fill** tab.
   c. Click a color darker than the background fill to add emphasis to the first row.

15 Select a font color for the Speaking row and the remaining rows that provides high contrast between the font color and the background colors. Use a different color the first row to add emphasis.

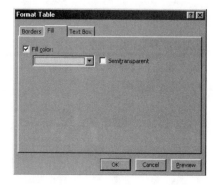

PowerPoint 97 users: The dialog box varies slightly from PowerPoint 2000, but the procedures are the same.

Creating Graphs

Well-designed, appealing graphs help the speaker convey quantitative information without overwhelming the audience. You will learn to enhance PowerPoint's basic default charts to create compelling bar charts and pie charts. You will also learn to change the chart type to be certain you have depicted the data in a logical manner for the decision maker.

Designer's Pointer

Powerful software programs such as PowerPoint produce highly professional graphics for oral presentations and written reports. However, selecting the graphic type that will depict data in the most effective manner is the important first decision you must make. Begin by identifying the primary idea you want the audience to understand related to your data. Then, choose an appropriate graphic type using these general guidelines:

Graphic Type	Objective
Table	Show exact figures
Bar chart (column or horizontal	Compare one quantity with another quantity
Line chart	Illustrate changes in quantities over time
Pie chart	Show how the parts of a whole are distributed

Input your data in PowerPoint's datasheet. Then view your data in several chart types until you identify the chart type that communicates your primary idea most effectively.

Creating a Column Chart

Study the enhanced chart and note the improvements over the two original graphics. The table is ineffective in communicating the relationship between the data in a simple manner. Taking the time to edit PowerPoint's basic defaults for a bar chart yields high dividends in overall appeal.

Directions: Follow the instructions to enhance the original slide as shown.

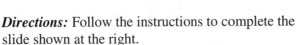

	After 3 Hours	After 3 days
Media Used		
Verbal	70	10
Visual	72	20
Verbal & visual	85	65

Increases Retention

**Ineffective Graphic Type to
Convey Data with Impact**

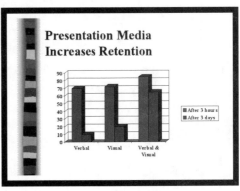

**Needs Improvement: Slide
Built with Defaults**

Directions: Follow the instructions to complete the slide shown at the right.

1   Create a new slide to appear after Slide 7 (Helps Speaker Accomplish Goals). Use the **Chart AutoLayout.**

2   Key the title in the title placeholder.

3   Omit the background object on this slide. (Click **Format, Background**. Click to remove the check in front of "Omit background graphics from master.")

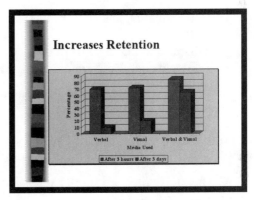

**Effective Column Chart
with Enhancements**

Select a Chart Type

4   Double click in the chart placeholder.

5   Click **Chart, Chart Type.**

6   Be sure the **Standard Types** tab is selected.

7   Click **Column** and select a chart type from the Chart Type dialog box.

8   Note the various types of column charts displayed in the gallery. Select the first column chart — clustered chart.

**Select sub-chart:
Clustered column**

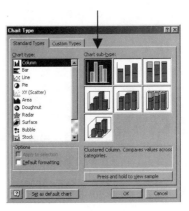

Edit the Sample Datasheet

9 Click in the first cell and input the data. Use the arrow keys to move to the next cell.

 ◄———— **Click to exit the datasheet**

		A	B	C	D	E
		Verbal	Visual	Verbal & Visual		
1	After 3 hou	70	72	85		
2	After 3 day	10	20	65		
3						
4						

10 Input all remaining data. Click **X** to exit the datasheet. To redisplay the datasheet for later revisions, click **View, Datasheet**.

Trouble Shooting Tip

If your chart has extra space to the right as shown in the illustration, you likely deleted the data but not the unneeded column in the datasheet. Follow these commands:

1. Drag and highlight the unneeded column(s) (Column D) and click **Edit, Delete, Entire Row**.
2. Drag and highlight the unneeded row(s) (Row 3) and click **Edit, Delete, Entire Row**.

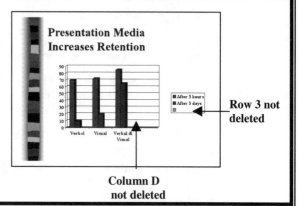

Row 3 not deleted

Column D not deleted

Input Title and Labels

11 Click **Chart, Chart Options, Titles**.

12 Input **Media Used** for the x-axis label.

13 Input **Percentage** for the z-axis (or y-axis) label.

Note: No title is added because the title will appear as the slide title.

FYI

To view the data in a different chart type, click **Chart, Chart Type**, and select a different chart type and sub-type.

Select Titles tab ———►

Input labels for x- and y-axis

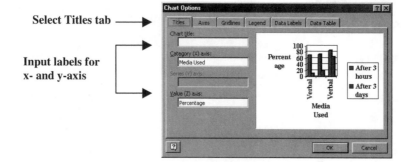

Format the Legend

14 Click **Chart, Chart Options, Legend**.

15 Click **Bottom**. The legend moves below the chart. This position allows space for increasing the size of the chart so that it can be seen clearly on a projected visual.

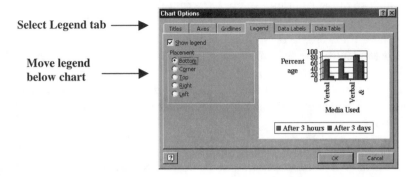

Select Legend tab ──→

Move legend
below chart ──→

Size the Chart

16 Hold down the **Shift** key, point to a corner handle and drag the chart. Enlarge the chart to occupy the space below the slide title allowing adequate even margins on all four sides.

Animate the Chart

17 Click **Slide Show, Custom Animation**.

18 Click the **Chart Effects** tab.

19 Select a **Wipe up effect** in the Entry Animation box. Click **Preview** and note the effect as the bars appear.

20 Select **by series** in the Introduce chart elements dialog box. Click **Preview** and note the "after 3 hours" bars come in first followed by the "after 3 days bars.

Note: The selection of a wipe up effect reinforces the idea that the use of multimedia (verbal and visual) increases retention both short-term and long-term.

21 Add a sound effect if you wish.

> **Trouble Shooting Tip**
> If you accidentally click off the chart and return to the slide, double click on the chart to return to the Chart Function. Attempt to resize your chart before you exit to the slide to avoid possible format problems.

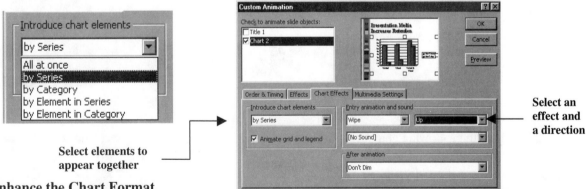

Select elements to
appear together

Select an
effect and
a direction

Enhance the Chart Format

You will make the following changes to enhance the appearance of the default column chart: Add a fill behind the chart area, increase the font size for easier readability of a projected visual, change the alignment of the y-axis label, and change the bar colors. Additionally, as you proceed through the menus, take the time to acquaint yourself with other ways column charts can be modified to increase appeal.

> **Trouble Shooting Tip**
> Two checkpoints to verify that you are in Chart Mode include (1) **Chart** is an option on the Menu toolbar and (2) a diagonal border surrounds around the chart.

22 Be sure you are in the Chart Mode and not in your slide.

23 Experiment with the use of the right mouse click to identify areas on the chart to format. Then, proceed to the next step to format the chart:

   a. Click near the part of the chart you wish to format (e.g., title, chart area, legend, axis labels). A prompt appears to identify the section of the chart you have selected. For example, a click slightly below the top border results in the selection of the Chart Area.

   b. As soon as a "Format _____ Area" prompt appears, right click and click, **Format** _____ (a part of the chart you designated appears; e.g., "Format Chart Area"). Input changes in the dialog box that appears.

FYI

You used the menu command (**Chart, Chart Options**) to move the legend below the chart. An alternate method is to use the convenient right click method you just learned. The Format Legend dialog box appears with three tabs for formatting the patterns, font, and placement. You can also right click to access Chart Type and Chart Options (commands on the Chart Menu). Experiment and choose the method that works best for you.

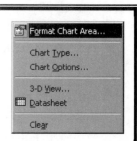

Add a Fill Behind the Chart

24 Point just inside the chart placeholder until the **Chart Area** prompt appears.

25 Right click, click **Format Chart Area**.

Chart Area Is Selected

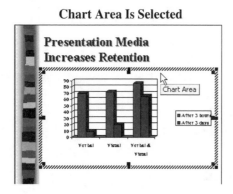

Format chart area →

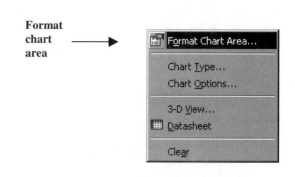

26 Make the following changes in the Format Chart Area dialog box.

   a. Click the **Patterns** tab.

   b. Select a line style, color, and weight.

   c. Select a fill color complimentary with the template.

Select Patterns tab →

Select line style color and weight →

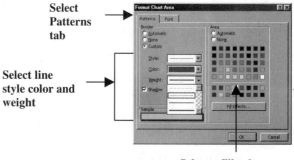

Select a fill color complimentary with template

d. Click the **Font** tab.

e. Change the font size to **20 points** to increase readability of the labels and values.

f. Note other changes that can be made: font face, font style, etc.

Select Font tab →

Change font size

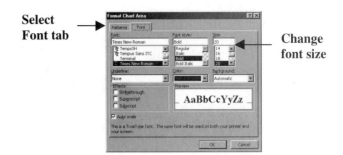

Change the Alignment of the Y-axis Label

27 Select the Value Axis Title area by clicking near the word *Percentage*. Refer to Steps 22-23 for instructions for selecting chart areas if necessary.

28 Right click and click **Format Axis Title**.

29 Click the **Alignment** tab

30 Point to the red arrow and drag until it is in the 12:00 position (from **0 to 90** degrees).
Note: To add a fill and/or border around the y-axis label or to edit the font, click the **Patterns** tab.

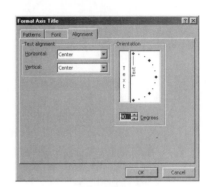

Change the Bar Colors

31 Select the second series of bars (after 3 days) by clicking on the second bar. Refer to Steps 22-23 if necessary.

32 Right click and click **Format Data Series**.

After 3 Days Bars Are Selected

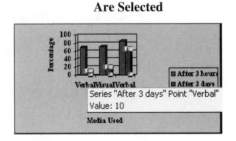

Format data series →

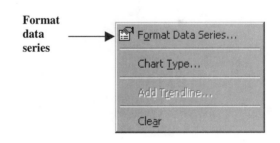

Designer's Pointer

Avoid using red and green as the colors of adjacent bars or pie slices. Almost 10 percent of the population are color impaired and cannot distinguish these two colors. Additionally avoid the use of red and green to differentiate between important points (green background and red text or red text on a green background).

33 Click the **Patterns** tab and select a fill color for the selected bars. Choose a color complimentary with the template that provides a high degree of contrast between the first series of bars.

Patterns tab
selected

Select border
color, style, and
weight

Select a fill color

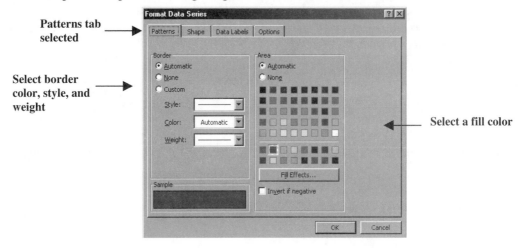

34 Click the other four tabs to acquaint yourself with the changes that can be made:
Shapes: Select one of six different shapes.
Data labels: Select to show the value above the bar.
Options: Make changes in the depth and width of the gap and the depth of the chart.

Shapes tab

Data Labels tab

Select a
shape for
the bars

Add value
above bar

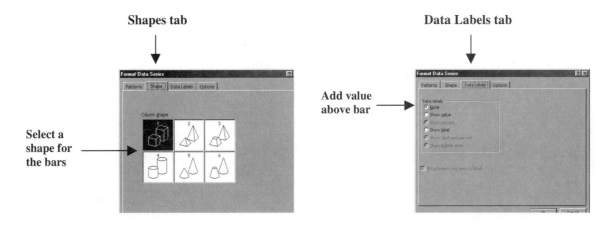

PowerPoint 97 users: The shapes of the bars cannot be changed in PowerPoint 97. Other minor variations exist in formatting the data series. Click the tabs to become acquainted with the options.

Creating a Pie Chart

Directions: Study the improvements in the enhanced slide and the original slide built using PowerPoint's defaults. Follow the instructions to enhance the original slide as shown.

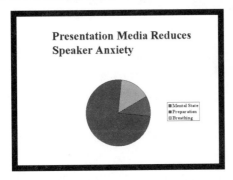

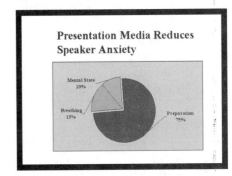

Slide Built with Defaults   Enhanced Slide

1   Create a new slide to appear after Slide 6 (Enhances Speaker's Delivery). Use the **Chart** AutoLayout.
2   Key the title in the title placeholder.
3   Omit the background object on this slide (Click **Format, Background**. Click to remove the check in front of "Omit background graphics from master.")

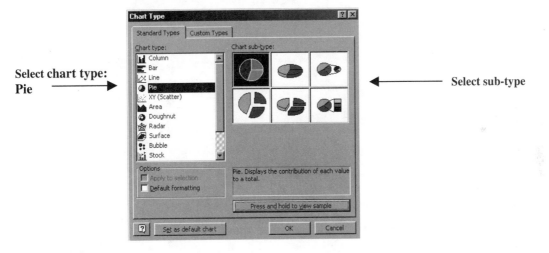

Select a Chart Type

4   Double click in the chart placeholder.
5   Click **Chart, Chart Type**.
6   Be sure the **Standard Types** tab is selected.
7   Click **Pie** from the Chart Type dialog box.
8   Note the various types of pie charts displayed in the gallery. Select the first pie chart.

Edit the Sample Datasheet

9   Click in the first cell and input the data. Use the arrow keys to move to the next cell.

10 Input all remaining data. Click **X** to exit the datasheet. To redisplay the datasheet for other revisions, click **View, Datasheet**.

11 Delete any unneeded rows and columns using the **Edit, Delete, Entire Column (Row)** command. Refer to the Trouble Shooting Tip on page 68 if necessary.

Input Chart Title

12 Do not include a title in the chart because the title will appear in the title placeholder. Should you wish to include the title in the chart, click **Chart, Chart Options**, and the **Titles** tab, and input the title.

Format the Labels

13 Click **Chart, Chart Options**.

14 Click the **Data Labels** tab.

15 Click **Show label and percent**. A preview slide appears to illustrate your selection — pie slice with label (Preparation) and value (75) and percent sign (%).

16 Click to remove the check before "Legend key next to label." Including a legend *and* the value and the percent beside the pie slide would be redundant.

17 Click to check **"Show leader lines."** Later you will move the labels away from the pie to display the leader lines.

Data labels tab selected

Select label & percent

Show leader lines but not legend

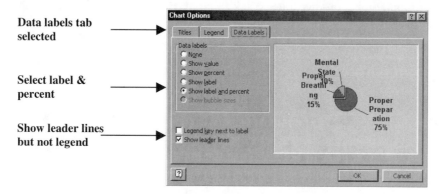

Omit Legend

18 Click **Chart, Chart Options**.

19 Click the **Legend** tab.

Omit legend

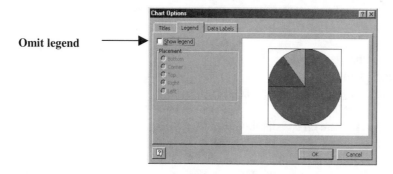

20 Click to remove the check in front of "Show Legend" box.

Animate the Chart

21   Click **Slide Show, Custom Animation**.

22   Click the **Chart Effects** tab.

23   Select **by category** in the Introduce Chart Elements dialog box.

24   Select a **Wipe Down effect** in the Entry Animation box. Click **Preview** and note the effect as the slices appear.

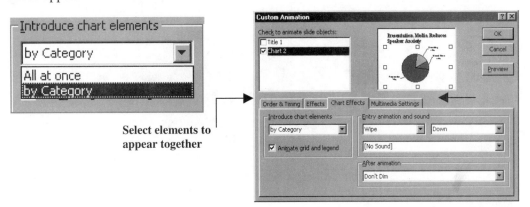

Select elements to
appear together

Select an
effect and
a direction

Enhance the Chart Format

You will make the following changes to enhance the appearance of the default pie chart: increase the size of the chart for added readability on a projected visual, change the angle of the pie slices to adhere to guidelines for constructing pie charts, change the slide colors, and explode the largest slice for added emphasis. Additionally, as you proceed through the menus, take the time to acquaint yourself with other ways pie charts can be modified to increase appeal.

25   Be sure you are in the Chart Mode and not in your slide.

26   Just as you did with the column chart, experiment with the use of the right mouse click to identify areas to be formatted. Then, proceed to the next step to format the chart:

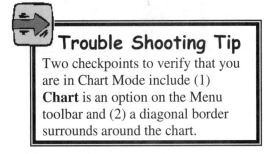

Trouble Shooting Tip

Two checkpoints to verify that you are in Chart Mode include (1) **Chart** is an option on the Menu toolbar and (2) a diagonal border surrounds around the chart.

   a.   Click near the part of the chart you wish to format (e.g., title, chart area, plot area, labels, etc.). A prompt will appear to identify the section of the chart you have selected. For example, a click slightly below the top border results in the selection of the Chart Area.

   b.   As soon as a "Format _____ Area" prompt appears, right click and click, **Format** _____ (a part of the chart you designated appears; e.g., "Format Chart Area"). Input changes in the dialog box that appears.

Size Chart

27   Point near the pie until you select the Plot Area. Hold down the **Shift** key as you drag the chart. Enlarge the chart to occupy the space below the slide title allowing adequate even margins on all four sides.

Plot Area Is Selected

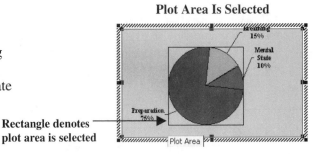

Rectangle denotes
plot area is selected

Delete Plot Marker

The rectangular border surrounding the Plot Area aids the designer in sizing the chart and identifying the plot area; it should not remain on the pie chart.

28 To remove this border:

    a. Select the Plot Area (border surrounds the pie as shown in the illustration above).

    b. Right click and click **Format Plot Area**.

    c. Click **None**.

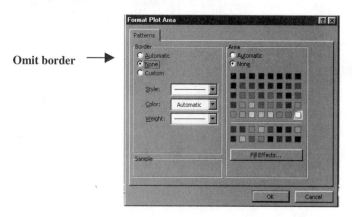

Change the Angle of the Slices

29 Click near the pie slices to select the Data Series area.

30 Click inside the angles box.

31 Press the spin arrow until the largest slice rotates to the 12 o'clock position.

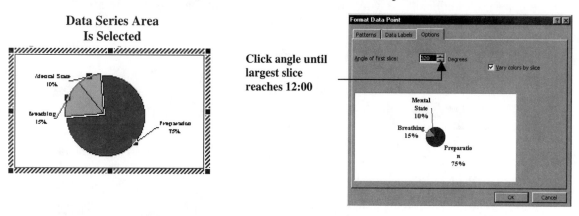

Add a Showcase Box Behind the Pie Chart

32 Point near the outside border of the chart and select Chart Area.

33 Right click and click Format Chart Area.

34 Click the **Patterns** tab and select a fill color and line color complimentary with the template.

Increase Font Size of Data Labels

35 Click near the data labels and select the Data Labels area.

36 Right click and click Format Data Labels.

37 Click the **Font** tab and change the font size to **20 points** to increase the readability of the labels.

Position the Data Labels and Add Leader Lines

38   Select one of the data labels and click until sizing handles appear.

39   Drag the slice away from the pie slide to a position that is appealing and readable. Note leader lines appear as you move the label away from the pie slice.

40   Reposition the labels of the other two slices as shown in the illustration.

One Data Label Is Selected

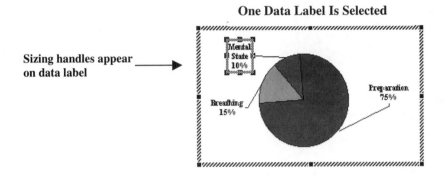

Sizing handles appear
on data label

Change the Slice Colors

41   Select the largest slice (Preparation).

42   Right click and click **Format Data Label (Preparation)**.

43   Click the **Patterns** tab and select a fill color. Choose a color complimentary with the template that provides a high degree of contrast between the other pie slices and the background behind the pie chart.

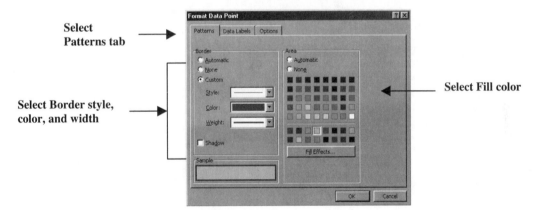

Select
Patterns tab

Select Border style,
color, and width

Select Fill color

Explode Slice for Emphasis

44   Select the largest slice (Preparation).

45   Drag until the slice moves away from the pie slightly — just enough to provide added emphasis to this slice. Refer to the model at the beginning of this activity.

Inserting a Slide Transition

Directions: Follow the instructions to add slide transitions to the slides created in this project.

1   Display the presentation in Slide Sorter view.

2   Select any slides that do not include a slide transition icon below the slide.

3   Click the **Slide Transition** button on the Slide Sorter toolbar

4   Select **Wipe Right** effect at a **Fast** speed setting.

   Note: This slide transition effect has been used for all other slides in this presentation except for Slide 10 (photograph as the background) and Slide 13 (The Speak Is the Star). These specimen slides require a more dramatic effect.

5   Click **Apply**.

Printing the Presentation

Directions: Print a copy of the file **Speak** as an audience handout with six slides per page. The slide should contain the following slides in order. Your instructor may instruct you to print the slides created in Project 6 only (highlighted slides).

1 Enhanced Title Slide
2 **Greatest Fears**
3 Effective Speakers
4 Average Presentation Rated
5 Keys to Effective Speaking
6 Enhances Speaker's Delivery
7 **Reduces Speaker's Anxiety**
8 Helps Speaker Accomplish Goals
9 **Increases Retention**
10 Makes Dollars and Sense
11 Selection Considerations
12 Common Problems with Visuals
13 The Speaker is the Star
14 Handling Hecklers
15 Converting Slides to Overheads
16 Photo as Slide Object (slide title and photos will vary)
17 The Speak Is the Star
18 Photo Background (photo will vary)

Project 7
Editing a Presentation and Rehearsing for Effective Delivery

Learning Objectives

➤ Design compelling coherence devices (agenda slide, summary slides, and divider slides) that assist the audience in moving smoothly through the organizational structure of a presentation.

➤ Use the speller and style checker to ensure accuracy in spelling and grammar and consistency in style.

➤ Use the rehearse timings feature to identify improvements while practicing delivery of a presentation.

Designing Coherence Devices

The Designer's Pointer outlines the importance of creating slides that aid in assuring a coherent presentation. In this project you will create (a) an agenda slide to preview major divisions of presentation, (b) a summary slide to preview divisions of a major point, and (c) divider slides to mark the beginning of the major points in a presentation.

Creating An Agenda Slide

A simple bulleted list listing your main points may convey the structure of your presentation. However, other creative techniques can help a speaker capture the audience's attention and set the stage for a dynamic presentation.

Directions: Study the sample agenda slides and begin generating other creative techniques for previewing the main points of your next presentation. Return to Project 5, page 57 to see the simple bulleted list that a novice designer might use for this critically important element in a presentation.

Designer's Pointer

A clear, logical organizational pattern for the content of a presentation is fundamental to an effective presentation. A writer includes headings to serve as signposts to mark the major and minor divisions of a report. Likewise, a speaker uses verbal cues to transition an audience through a presentation smoothly. These cues include a preview of the main points to be covered prior to moving into the body of the presentation and transition words such as *first, next, finally*. These cues can be incorporated into slides that aid in developing a smooth, coherent presentation.

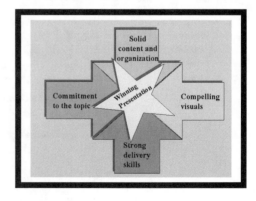

Sample Agenda Slides

1 Be sure the file **Speak** is open.
2 Complete *one* of the following activities as directed by your instructor:
   a. Redesign Slide 5 (Keys to Effective Speaking), the agenda slide for the file **Speak,** using the four arrows illustrated in the model or using a creative technique of your own.
   b. Create an agenda slide using the main points of a presentation you are currently developing. Position this slide as the last slide in the presentation.

Creating A Summary Slide

Creating a simple bulleted list that serves as a preview of the content of upcoming slides is easy using PowerPoint's summary slide feature. This feature is especially useful to create a slide that will preview the subpoints supporting a major point.

Directions: Follow the instructions to create a summary slide entitled *Slide Design Guidelines* that lists the four points to be covered in this major section of a presentation.

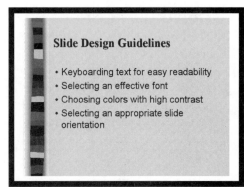

Create the Slides to Be Included on the Summary Slide

1 Create four new slides to appear after Slide 12 (Common Problems with Visuals). Use the **Bulleted List** AutoLayout.
2 Key the titles in the title placeholder of each slide:
   Keyboarding Text for Readability
   Selecting an Effective Font
   Choosing Colors with High Contrast
   Select Appropriate Slide Orientation
   Note: If you wish to complete these entire slides, refer to the directions at the end of this project.

Select the Slides to Be Included on the Summary Slide

3 Hold down the **Shift** key as you click to select the four slides you just created.
4 In the Slide Sorter view, click the **Summary Slide** button. A new slide appears in front of the first selected slide. The slide title is *Summary Slide*, and the titles of the four selected slides make up the four bulleted items.

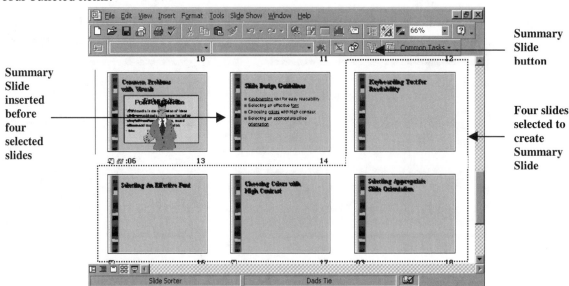

5   Display the summary slide in Normal or Slide view.

6   Edit the title to be **Slide Design Guidelines**.

7   Reformat the text to fit the bulleted list placeholder. For example, text displayed in two lines on the slide title can be fit on one line.

8   Change the capitalization style so only the first word in the bulleted items is capitalized:
    PowerPoint 2000:   Click the light bulb and click **Sentence case**.
    PowerPoint 97:   Highlight the bulleted list. Click **Format, Change Case, Sentence case**.

Add a Slide Transition

9   Click the **Slide Transition** button on the Slide Sorter toolbar

10   Select **Wipe right** as the slide transition for consistency with other slides in the presentation.

Creating Divider Slides

A divider slide is positioned at the beginning of each major point of a presentation to remind the audience where the speaker is in the organization structure and to target attention to this new discussion.

Directions: Study the Designer's Pointer below. Develop a standard design for the divider slides to be used throughout the presentation **Speak**. Follow the design suggestions provided or use your own creative techniques.

Create a Master Divider Slide

1   Create a new slide at the beginning of the presentation. Select one of the following AutoLayouts:
    — **Title Only** — if you intend to include an image on each divider slide.
    — **Title Slide** — if the template image will be the only image on these slides.

2   Select the patterned background you used on the enhanced title slide or a background of your choice.

3   Add a slide transition that is slightly more dramatic than the Wipe Right used in the other slides. Because you're adding the slide transition to the master, the same slide transition will be used consistently on all divider slides.

4   Add a subtle sound on the slide transition. (e.g., chime, sparkle).

Copy the Master to Create Each Divider Slide

5   Go to the Slide Sorter view and duplicate the divider slide master (select the slide and click **Edit, Copy** and then **Edit, Paste** or press **Ctrl-D**).

6   Move the copy of the Master Divider Slide to follow Slide 5 (Keys to Effective Speaking) and display in Normal view.

Designer's Pointer

To achieve the goal of directing the audience through a presentation, the divider slides (three or four slides depending on the number of points) in a presentation should be compelling.

- Include on each divider slide a descriptive title that engages the audience's attention and perhaps an image that reinforces the major idea.

- Select a slightly different color scheme and perhaps a different fill effect (e.g., patterns, texture) that is complimentary with the presentation template but that the audience will clearly identify as the signposts marking a new section.

- Consider selecting a subtle, relevant sound effect to bring added emphasis to this turning point in your presentation. A subtle sound will not be distracting since the presentation will only have a few divider slides.

If time is limited, you might select the title AutoLayout for the divider slide. Thus, the title is centered and the slide master object positioned differently than in other layouts.

7   Input the title in the placeholder: **Why Use Presentation Media** (substitute a title of your choice if you would like).

8   Incorporate relevant images (optional).

9   Insert another copy of the Master Divider Slide after Slide 11 (Makes Dollars & Sense).

10 Input the title in the placeholder: **Designing Compelling Visuals** (substitute a title of your choice if you would like). Incorporate images (optional).

Proofreading a Slide Show

A speaker will lose credibility instantly if slides contain spelling and grammatical errors. A systematic plan for proofreading includes using PowerPoint's Speller to locate spelling errors and Style Checker to ensure consistency in several styles.

Using the Speller

Follow the instructions to check the spelling in the file **Speak**.

1   Click **Tools, Spelling**.

2   Click to select the appropriate correction from the Spelling dialog box that appears when a spelling error is detected:

   a. Click **Change** to accept a recommended spelling.

   b. Click the correct spelling from the list provided and then click **Change**.

   c. Click **Ignore all** instances of a word if a word is spelling correctly but is marked because the word is not in PowerPoint's dictionary. You may also click "Add words to" to add the word to the dictionary.

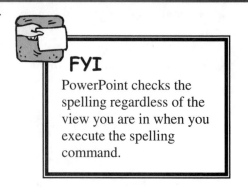

FYI

PowerPoint checks the spelling regardless of the view you are in when you execute the spelling command.

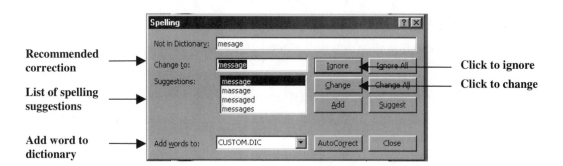

3   Save the presentation to add these corrections to the file.

Using the Style Checker

In addition to checking spelling, the Style Checker checks for visual clarity and case and end punctuation. Because of enhancements to PowerPoint 2000, instructions are provided for PowerPoint 2000 and PowerPoint 97.

PowerPoint 2000

PowerPoint 2000 automatically checks your presentation for consistency and style and marks problems on a slide with a light bulb. Follow these instructions for correcting a problem on a slide:

Correct Detected Problems

1   Be sure the Office Assistant is turned on. Click **Help, Office Assistant**.
2   Click the light bulb, and then click the appropriate option.
3   Note in the illustration, PowerPoint recognizes an inconsistency in the capitalization of a bulleted list and displayed the prompt shown. The designer clicks "Change the text to sentence case" to capitalize the word *Reduces*.

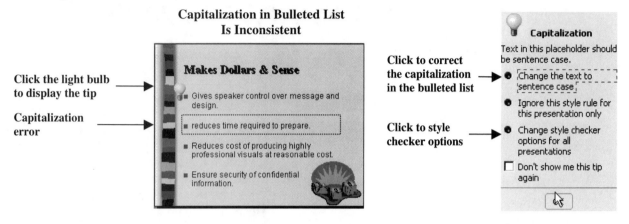

Click the light bulb to display the tip

Capitalization error

Click to correct the capitalization in the bulleted list

Click to style checker options

PowerPoint 97

1   Click **Tools, Style Checker**.
2   Select the elements to be checked from the Style Checker dialog box.

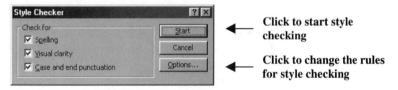

Click to start style checking

Click to change the rules for style checking

3   Click **Start** to begin the checking process.
4   Respond to the prompts displayed when PowerPoint detects an error.
    Note the prompt displayed when PowerPoint detected end punctuation in a bulleted list (shown below).

Contains End Punctuation
Following Bulleted List

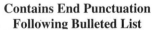

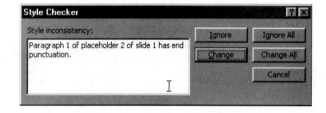

Rehearsing a Presentation

The Rehearse Timing features records the actual time of the presentation and the time spent on each slide. Use this information to edit your presentation (a) to locate errors in logical development and flow, smooth transition from one point to the next, and content and (2) enhance your delivery skills.

Setting Rehearsal Timings

Directions: Follow the instructions to use the rehearsal timings to practice delivering your presentation.

1   Go to Slide Sorter view and click the **Rehearse Timing** button on the Slide Sorter toolbar. The slide show automatically goes into the Slide Show view.

    PowerPoint 97 users: Click **Slide Show, Rehearse Timings** or click the Rehearse Timings button on the Slide Sorter toolbar.

Presenter's Tip

Use the timing for total time spent in the presentation to ensure that your presentation fits a required time slot. For example, take a look at slides with extremely long timings. Perhaps these slides should be divided because they contain too much information or perhaps these timings reflect content that is tripping you up — you just have not yet determined how to present the content concisely.

Rehearse Timings

2   Advance through the presentation **Speak** as if you were the speaker delivering the actual presentation. Use the buttons in the Rehearsal dialog box superimposed on the slide to refine your delivery:
    a. Click **Repeat** to reset the clock so you can delivery the slide again.
    b. Click **Pause** to stop the clock as you review your notes, rethink your discussion, etc.
    c. Click **Next** to move to the next slide.

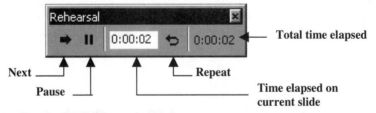

Next ——   Total time elapsed
Pause ——   Repeat
              Time elapsed on
              current slide

3   Continue until you have reached the last slide in the presentation and the following dialog box appears.

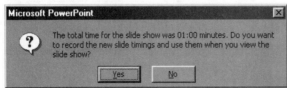

4   Click **Yes** to record the new slide timings. The slides are displayed in Slide Sorter view with the timings for individual slides displayed below each slide. Review the sample slides with timings provided in the following illustration.

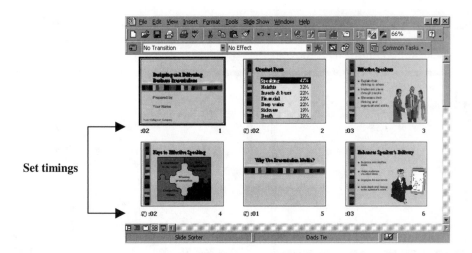

Set timings

Running a Slide Show With Rehearsal Timings

With the settings recorded on the slide show (as shown in the previous illustration), you can run a presentation with the set timings or run the slide show manually.

Directions: Follow the instructions to use the rehearsal timings to run a presentation manually and with set timings.

1   **Click Slide Show, Set Up Show.**
2   Note the two selections in the Set up Show dialog box:
   a.   Click **Manually** to advance the slide on a mouse click.
   b.   Click **Using timings, if present** to allow the slides to advance automatically using the set timings.

Advance slides manually

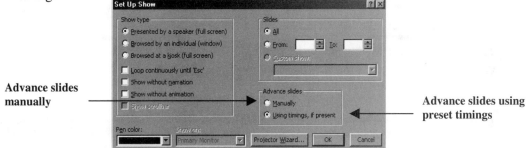

Advance slides using preset timings

PowerPoint 97 users: The Set Up Show menu looks slightly different but contains similar options.

3   Run the presentation **Speak** using the set timings. Run the show a second time using the manual setting.

Presenter's Tip

Setting timings is essential when designing automated presentations that will be run at exhibit areas or sent to potential customers/clients with narration replacing a human speaker. You can use set timings as you rehearse to help you maintain the pace needed to fit a predetermined time slot. However, run the presentation manually during your actual presentation because preset timings on all slides will diminish a speaker's ability to adapt the presentation to the audience's needs and to entertain questions, manage interruptions, etc.

Completing Slides 17—20

Directions: Complete Slides 17–20 (shown below) if directed to do so. Use your judgment to animate the slides to achieve the desired control over the text.

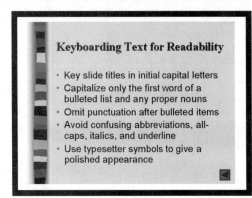

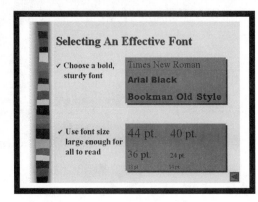

Slide 17   Slide 18

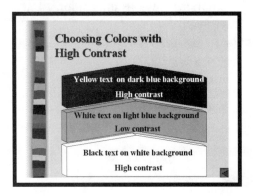

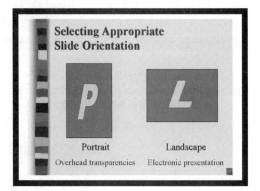

Slide 19   Slide 20

Printing the Presentation

Directions: Print a copy of the file **Speak** as an audience handout with six slides per page. The slide should contain the following slides in order. Your instructor may instruct you to print the slides created in Project 7 only (highlighted slides).

1	Enhanced Title Slide	13	Selection Considerations
2	Greatest Fears	14	Common Problems with Visuals
3	Effective Speakers	15	Handling Hecklers
4	Average Presentation Rated	16	**Slide Design Principles**
5	Keys to Effective Speaking	17	**Keyboarding Text for Readability**
6	**Why Use Presentation Media**	18	**Selecting an Effective Font**
7	Enhances Speaker's Delivery	19	**Choosing Colors with High Contrast**
8	Reduces Speaker Anxiety	20	Selecting Appropriate Slide Orientation
9	Helps Speaker Accomplish Goals	21	**Converting Slides to Overheads**
10	Increases Retention	22	Photo as Slide Object (slide title and photo will vary)
11	Makes Dollars and Sense	23	The Speaker Is the Star
12	**Designing Compelling Visuals**	24	Photo Background (photo will vary)

Project 8
Developing Useful Speaker's Notes and Professional Audience Handouts

Learning Objectives
➢ Create speaker's notes designed to aid a speaker during delivery.
➢ Create professional audience handouts that enhance the credibility of a speaker.

Constructing Useful Speaker's Notes Pages

PowerPoint can be used to construct useful notes pages that aid the speaker during delivery. You will learn two methods: (1) Adding speaker notes while running the presentation for practice purposes and (2) inserting notes directly in the Notes Pane of the Normal view in PowerPoint 2000 or the Notes Pages view in PowerPoint 97.

Adding Speaker's Notes While Rehearsing

Directions: Follow the instructions to create speaker's notes for one slide in the presentation **Speak**. Print a copy to submit to your instructor.

1 Begin running the presentation **Speak** in Slide Show view.
2 Right click when you have advanced to Slide 3 (Effective Speakers) — the slide where you will input speaker's notes.
3 Click **Speaker's Notes** from the menu.
4 Key notes in the Speaker Notes dialog.

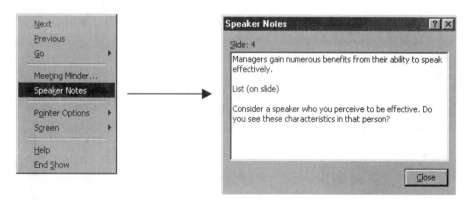

Edit Notes in the Notes Pane
5 Press **Escape** and display Slide 2 in the Normal view (or Notes Pages view for PowerPoint 97). *Note:* The text keyed while running the presentation in Slide Show view has been inserted in the Notes Pane (text area of the Notes Pages view in PowerPoint 97). See the illustration on the next page.
6 Select all the text in the placeholder by holding **Ctrl** and pressing **A** (**Ctrl-A**).
7 Increase the font size to at least 14 points so that the notes can be read easily in a darkened room (adjust the size of the print to a speaker's needs for a specific presentation).
8 Revise the notes if necessary. Add emphasis where needed (boldface, bulleted lists).

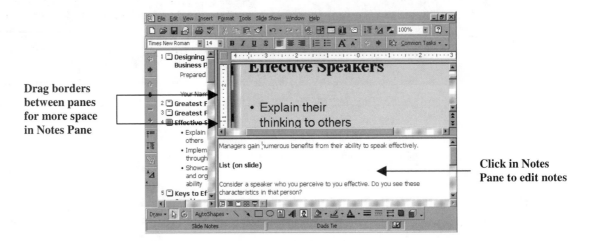

Drag borders between panes for more space in Notes Pane

Click in Notes Pane to edit notes

9   Continue to the next section.

Presenter's Tip

Surprisingly, rather than overrelying on notes, speakers frequently rely on notes less than they should. Under speaking pressure, speakers panic at the sight of dense, poorly prepared notes and thus, attempt to deliver the presentation with no aid at all or read a complete script rather than deliver the speech extemporaneously. Preparing useful speaker's notes will reduce speaker anxiety and enhance a speaker's delivery. Follow these guidelines for developing the content and format of useful speaker's notes to support your next presentation:

Content: Use trigger statements that prompt you to remember the next point and that highlight the logical flow of the slide. Include additional detail for content that demands precision and accuracy; for example, the introduction and conclusion, statistics, quotations, a joke or humorous story with a punch line.

Format: Design notes so they (a) appear uncluttered with plenty of white space and a uniform structure (bulleted list, outline); (b) are printed in large, easy-to-read font; (c) are printed on large pages that can be turned without distraction and numbered so they can be reordered quickly if they are dropped or mishandled; and (d) are neat with no last-minute confusing revisions, such as arrows denoting major reordering of ideas that won't be understood while under pressure.

Adding Speaker's Notes in the Notes Pane

Directions: Create speaker's notes for one slide in the presentation **Speak** (or **Speakrev**). Follow the guidelines provided in the Presenter's Tip. Print a copy to submit to your instructor.

1   Display a slide of your choice in Normal view.
     PowerPoint 97 users: Display slide in Notes Pages view.
2   Set the **Zoom** at 66% so that the text can be read easily.
3   Key the text — a few trigger statements to prompt your thoughts and remind you of the logical flow of the discussion on this slide. Review the guidelines for writing useful speaker's notes.
4   Select all the text in the placeholder by holding **Ctrl and pressing A** (**Ctrl-A**).

5   Increase the font size to at least 14 points so that the notes can be read easily in a darkened room (adjust the size to fit a speaker's needs for a specific presentation).

6   Continue to the next section.

Adding a Header and a Footer to the Notes Pages

Directions: Add a header and a footer to the notes pages of the presentation **Speak**. Print a copy to present to your instructor.

1   Click **View, Header and Footer**.

2   Be sure the **Notes and Handouts** tab is selected.

3   Edit the Header and Footer dialog box:

   a. Be sure slide number box is checked. A page number will appear on each notes page.

   b. Click **Header** and input the title of the presentation in the dialog box: **Designing and Delivering Business Presentations**.

   c. Click **Footer** and input in the dialog box: **Presented by Your Name**.

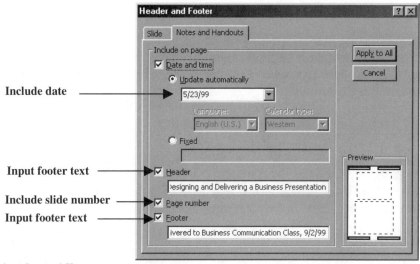

4   Click **Apply to All**.

Print Notes Page for Slide 2 and Slide of Your Choice

5   Click **File**, **Print**.

6   Edit the Print dialog box:

   a. Select **Slides** in the Print Range box and input 2 and the slide number of the slide of your choice.

   b. Select **Notes Pages** in the Print what box.

7   Click **OK**.

Note: Do not save your file. Proceed directly to the next section.

Creating Professional Audience Handouts

Audience handouts must reflect the same degree of professionalism as the slide show and the speaker's delivery. Create professional handouts that increase a speaker's credibility using two methods: (a) Add a header and footer to the master audience handout and (2) create a formal handout by exporting the slides to Word and inputting extensive commentary to supplement the slides.

Editing the Handout Master

Directions: Follow the instructions to change the format of the handout master for the presentation **Speak**. You will be instructed to print a copy to present to your instructor.

1   Close the presentation file **Speak** without saving changes. Open the file again.

2   Click **View, Master, Handout Master**.

   Note: Text will be added to the four placeholders on the handout master (shown on the illustration).

Edit the Four Placeholders

3   Header

   a. Click in the header placeholder and input the title of the presentation: **Designing and Delivering Business Presentations**.

   b. Select a font face of your choice and set the font size to **9 points** and **bold face**.

   c. Resize placeholder so the text appears on one line.

Date

   a. Click in the data area.

   b. Highlight the text that appears in the placeholder (Date/Time) and format the text to match the text in the header area. See the FYI feature box on the next page for a shortcut for formatting this text.

Footer

   a. Click in the footer placeholder and input: **Prepared by Your Name**. Press **Enter** and key the following text on the next line**: The title of the course you are taking that requires you to complete this presentation**.

   b. Format the text to match the text in the other placeholders. See the FYI feature box on the next page for a shortcut for formatting this text.

Page Number Area

   a. Click in the page number placeholder.

   b. Input the word *Page* before the text that appears in the placeholder (#). Highlight the text and format to match the text in the other three placeholders.

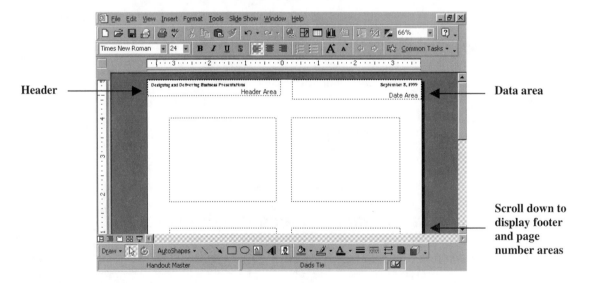

Print Notes Page for Slides 1–3

4   Click **File, Print**.

5   Edit the Print dialog box:

   a. Select **Slides** in the Print Range box and input **1-3**.

   b. Select **Handouts** in the Print what box and select **3** per page.

6   Click **OK**.

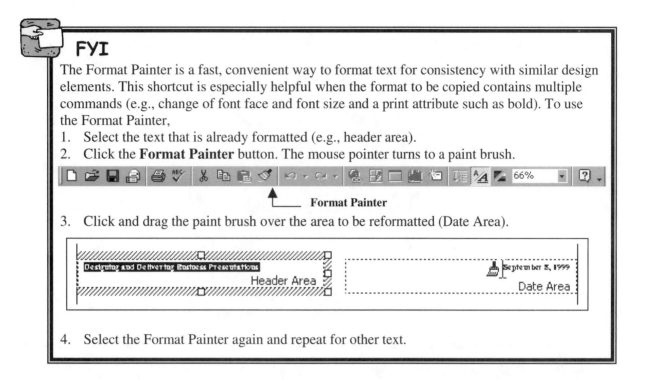

FYI

The Format Painter is a fast, convenient way to format text for consistency with similar design elements. This shortcut is especially helpful when the format to be copied contains multiple commands (e.g., change of font face and font size and a print attribute such as bold). To use the Format Painter,

1. Select the text that is already formatted (e.g., header area).
2. Click the **Format Painter** button. The mouse pointer turns to a paint brush.

Format Painter

3. Click and drag the paint brush over the area to be reformatted (Date Area).

4. Select the Format Painter again and repeat for other text.

Creating Audience Handouts Using the Send to Word Feature

Directions: Follow the instructions to export the presentation file **Speak** to Word and then input speaker notes in the available space.

1 Click the **Grayscale Preview** button on the Standard toolbar. This command converts your presentation to black and white. Omit this step if you intend to print your handout with a color printer.

Grayscale Preview ——

PowerPoint 97 users: This button is referred to as the *Black & White View* but is in the same location as in PowerPoint 2000.

2 Click **File, Send to, Microsoft Word**.

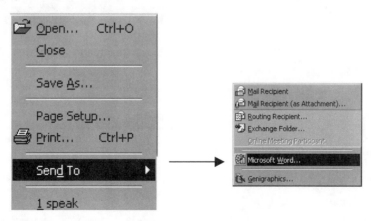

3 Study the five available layouts: notes next to slides, blank lines next to slides, notes below slides, blank lines below slides, and outline only.

4   Select **Notes next to slides**. Any notes keyed in the text area on the Notes Pages View will appear in a notes column next to the related slide.

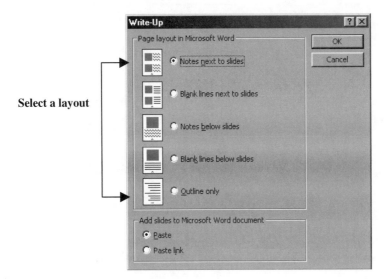

Select a layout

Designer's Pointer

The notes next-to-slides format allows you to insert supplementary notes next to your slide. Microsoft automatically formats a highly professional "take home package" for an audience who will be responsible for the material covered in the presentation, such as seminar participants of required training programs. Additionally, the commentary will aid persons who cannot attend the presentation but is responsible for the material or who simply wishes to benefit from the presentation.

5   Wait patiently as your presentation is exported to Microsoft Word and formatted into a three-column table.
   Note: Text should appear beside two slides — the notes you keyed in a previous activity.

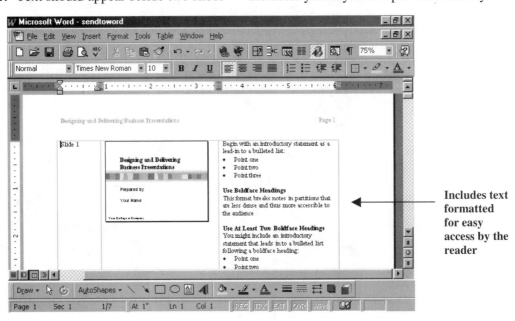

Includes text formatted for easy access by the reader

6   Save this Word document as **Speak.doc**. Note the file size is extremely large because the file is graphics intensive.

Delete Unneeded Slides

7   Select the row containing Slide 2 (Greatest Fears) by clicking in the first column and dragging across to highlight the entire column. Alternately, click anywhere in the row and click **Table, Select Row**. *Note:* Slide 2 is useful for establishing the purpose of the presentation but is not necessary for inclusion in a formal audience handout.

8   Click Table, **Delete Cells**
9   Click **Delete entire row** from the Delete Cells dialog box. The row is deleted and the other slides move up to fill the space.

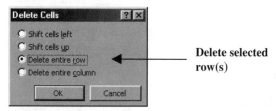

Delete selected row(s)

10   Repeat the procedure to delete other necessary slides (e.g., the photo that contains the photo background).

Designer's Pointer

Include in a formal audience handout only the slides you anticipate the audience will need for later reference. For example, exclude dramatic opening or closing slides used to capture the audience's attention and other graphic-intensive slides that contain little text and will not be meaningful outside the presentation. Take a close look at unneeded slides if you have one slide printing on the last page.

Inputting Supplementary Notes to a Send to Word Handout

Directions: Follow the instructions to input supplementary notes to one slide.

1   Click in the notes column to the right of a slide (third column) of your choice. Key notes that will aid the audience in understanding the slide even if the person was not present. Use the format tips described in the illustration on page 92 to avoid dense, unappealing text.
2   Scroll to display the text for the two slides you added earlier. Change the format to match the format of the notes you input directly in the Word document if necessary.
3   Continue to the next section to complete the Send to Word handout.

Adding a Header and a Footer to a Send to Word Handout

Directions: Follow the instructions to add a header and a footer to the presentation **Speak**. You will be instructed to print a copy to present to your instructor.

Insert a Header

1   Click **View, Header and Footer**.
2   Click in the header placeholder and input text in the title of the presentation: **Designing and Delivering Business Presentations**.
3   Press **Tab** until the cursor reaches the end of the placeholder. Key the text: **Page.**

Presenter's Tip

Adding an appealing header/footer to a top-notch handout increases a speaker's credibility as a competent person in the specific area being discussed. Also, the complete identification (name, company, and date) serves as an advertisement for a presenter and his/her company.

4   Click **Insert Page Number** in the Header and Footer dialog box. The number 1 appears to the right of the word *Page* and changes as you move through the pages of the document.

5   Click the **Format Page Number** button and key a value if you wish to start numbering with a value other than 1.

6   Highlight all text in the header placeholder. Format with a font face of your choice and a font size of **9 points** and **bold face**.

7   Click **Switch Between Header and Footer** to move to the footer placeholder at the bottom of the page.

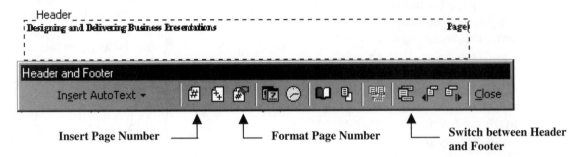

Insert a Footer

8   Click in the footer placeholder and input the text: **Prepared by your name and name of your university/company.**

9   Press **Tab** until the cursor reaches the end of the placeholder. Key the text: **Current Date.**

10 Highlight all text in the header placeholder. Format this text to match the header. Use the Format Painter feature you used previously in this project to ensure consistency in the design.

11 Click **Close** to exit the header and footer area and return to the document.

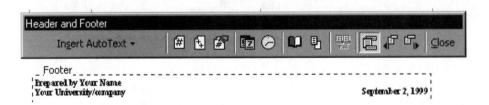

Print Send to Word Handout

12 Click **File, Print**.

13 Click **OK**.

Project 9
Making a Presentation Interactive

Learning Objectives

➢ Hide a slide that can be accessed conveniently should the information be needed during a presentation.
➢ Create a hyperlink to a web site on the Internet.
➢ Create a hyperlink accessed by moving the mouse over the hyperlink.
➢ Create a series of hyperlinks accessed from a summary slide.
➢ Create a link to a Microsoft Excel notebook for the purpose of automatically updating a chart in PowerPoint.
➢ Apply design techniques that foster audience involvement.

Adding Interactivity to Slides

Experienced speakers recognize the importance of adapting a presentation in response to feedback received from an audience during an actual presentation. Hidden slides and hyperlinks are two powerful PowerPoint features that build flexibility into a presentation. The speaker can move through a presentation in sequences other than the typical linear pattern from the first slide to the last slide and launch other applications (e.g., notebook file or an Internet browser) in a seamless, effortless manner. In addition to hiding slides and creating hyperlinks, you will learn creative techniques designed to foster audience involvement.

Hiding a Slide

A hidden slide allows you to customize a slide show for a particular audience. You simply mark slides you don't want to project unless the information on the slide is needed during a presentation. A speaker might include on a hidden slide detailed data needed to substantiate a point in a presentation in anticipation that an audience member might ask for further explanation of this point.

Directions: Follow the instructions to hide specific slides and to project the hidden slides during the presentation.

Hide a Slide

1 Display the file **Speak** in the Slide Sorter view.
2 Select Slide 21 (Converting Slides to Overheads) and Slide 22 (Photo as Slide Object).
3 Click the **Hide Slide** button on the Slide Sorter toolbar. A diagonal line appears over the slide number to indicate the slide is hidden.

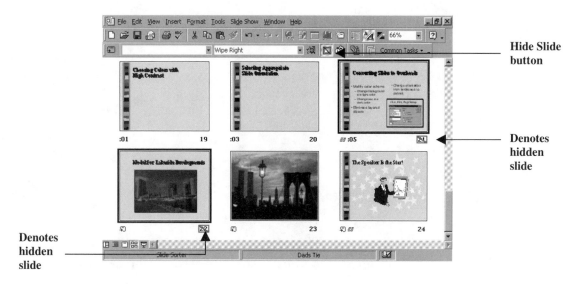

4   Select Slide 20 (Selecting Appropriate
     Slide Orientation); this slide
     immediately precedes the hidden slide.

5   Click the **Slide Show view** button to
     begin running the presentation.

6   Click the mouse once. Note Slide 23 is
     displayed; Slides 21 and 22 are
     skipped because they are hidden.

Unhide a Slide

1   Select Slide 22 (Photo as Slide Object)
     in the Slide Sorter view.

2   Click the **Hide Slide** button on the
     Slide Sorter toolbar. The diagonal line
     over the slide number is removed.

View a Hidden Slide

1   Select Slide 20 (Selecting Appropriate Slide Orientation); this slide immediately precedes the
     hidden slide (Slide 21, Converting Slides to Overheads).

2   Click the **Slide Show view** button to begin running the presentation.

3   Press the letter **H** to advance to the hidden slide.

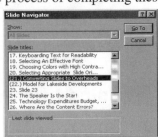

Presenter's Tip

Another way to view the hidden slide is to right click and click **Go, Slide Navigator**. The slide number of a hidden slide is enclosed in parentheses in the list of titles. Using the keyboard command is preferable because it facilitates a seamless delivery. The process of completing these mouse clicks and the display of several unattractive drop-down menus draw attention away from the speaker and toward the technology.

Creating Hyperlinks

A *hyperlink* is an area of the screen the speaker can click to move automatically to a variety of locations. In this project you will create hyperlinks to (1) access a web site, (2) move to a specific slide within a presentation, and (3) open a Microsoft Excel notebook. Hyperlinks can also be added to move to a different PowerPoint presentation and numerous other locations.

Adding a Hyperlink to a Web Site

Directions: Follow the instructions to create a hyperlink to a web site.

Insert Hyperlink

1   Display Slide 1 in Normal view.

2   Highlight either your name or the name of your university/company.

3   Click **Insert, Hyperlink**.

4   Input the URL address of your personal home page or university/company web site. Follow the
     format shown in the illustration. Click **OK**.

PowerPoint 2000   **PowerPoint 97**

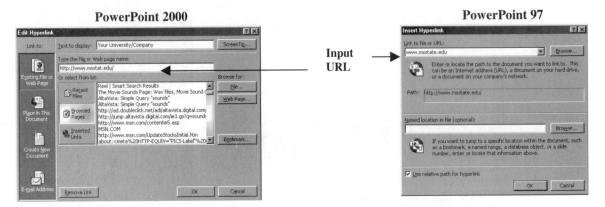

Input
URL

5   Note the text you highlighted in Step 2 is now displayed in a different color.

Access the Hyperlink to Verify Accuracy

6   Display the presentation in Slide Show view.
Note: You must be running the presentation to access a hyperlink.

7   Click the hyperlink (words accented in a different color).
Note: The hand pointer appears as you move over the hyperlinked words. Then, the Internet browser opens and connects to the appropriate web site.

8   Click the **Exit** or **Minimize** button in the Internet browser to return to the slide show.

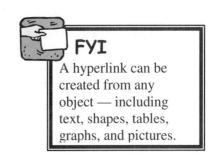

FYI

A hyperlink can be created from any object — including text, shapes, tables, graphs, and pictures.

Select Color of Hyperlink Text Before Hyperlink Has Been Accessed

9   Click, **Format, Slide Color Scheme**.
10   Click the **Custom** tab.
11   Click **Accent and hyperlink**, **Change Color**.
12   Select a color from the **Standard** or **Custom** tab.

Select Color of Hyperlink Text After Hyperlink Has Been Visited

13   Repeat Steps 9–10.
14   Click **Accent and followed hyperlink**, **Change Color**.
15   Select a color from the **Standard** or **Custom** tab.

Before visit

After visit

Hyperlinking Using the Mouse Over Technique

Directions: Follow the instructions to create a hyperlink to a specific slide accessed by moving the mouse over the hyperlinked object rather than clicking the mouse.

Insert a Hyperlink

1   Display Slide 22 (Photo as a Slide Object) in Normal view.

2   Click to select the photograph.

3   Click **Slide Show, Action Settings**.

4   Select the **Mouse Over** tab at the top of the dialog box.
Note: The mouse click is the default method for accessing a hyperlink.

5   Click the **Hyperlink to** option and the list arrow.

6   Click **Next Slide**.

Select Mouse Over tab

Click Hyperlink to

Select Next Slide

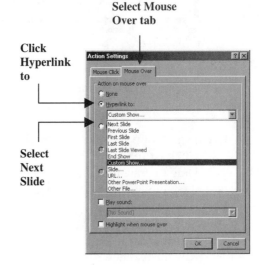

Access the Hyperlink

7   Display the presentation in Slide Show view.

8   Drag the mouse across the photo without clicking. The slide will advance to the next slide (Slide 23, The Speaker Is the Star).

Trouble Shooting Tip

You cannot add a hyperlink to a grouped object. Thus, if you add a showcase box (AutoShape with enhancements) behind the photo, do not group the two objects.

Creating Hyperlinks on a Summary Slide

Adding hyperlinks to buttons makes hyperlinks transparent; thus, attention remains directed toward the speaker and the message—unlike the obvious underlined hyperlinks illustrated in the original slide. Hyperlink buttons are dynamic and appealing, and the audience is unaware of the presence of a hyperlink until the speaker accesses it.

Directions: Follow the instructions to enhance the original slide and to create four hyperlinks that will allow you to jump to specific slides in the presentation **Speak**. You will create (a) a hyperlink from each button to a specific slide in the presentation and (2) return hyperlinks to jump back to the summary slide.

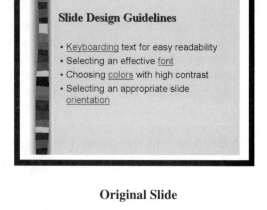

Original Slide

Summary Slide with Hyperlink Buttons

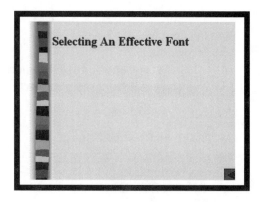

Hyperlink Returning to the Summary Slide

1 Display Slide 16 (Slide Design Guidelines).
2 Delete the bulleted list placeholder.

Create a Design for the Hyperlink Buttons
3 Click **AutoShapes, Basic Shapes, Bevel**.
4 Drag to draw the button. When you release the mouse the button is selected (note the sizing handles in the illustration below).
5 Size the button allowing space for four buttons to appear attractively on the slide.
6 Key the text describing the first hyperlink in the textbox: **Keyboarding Rules**.
7 Format the text:
   a. Center the text in the button.
   b. Select an appealing font face and font size that fits in the button but is large enough to be read easily. Add effects such as bold or shadow if you wish.

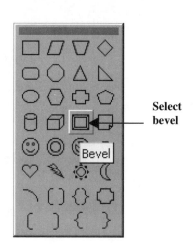

Select bevel

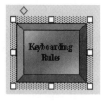

Create the Remaining Buttons Using the Copy Feature to Ensure Consistency

Copied Buttons Before Editing

8 Select the completed button and hold down Ctrl as you drag the button. An icon with a plus sign appears as you drag the slide indicating an object is being moved.

9 Drop the button on the slide.

10 Repeat steps 8–9 to create two additional buttons.

11 Edit the text in each copied button to create the following four buttons:

Top left:	Keyboarding Rules (already keyed)
Top right:	Font Selection
Bottom left:	Color Choice
Bottom right:	Orientation

Insert the Hyperlinks

12 Click to select the first button (Keyboarding Rules).

13 Click **Slide Show, Action Settings**.

14 Be sure the **Mouse Click** tab is selected.

15 Click **Hyperlink to** option and click the list arrow.

16 Click **Slide**.

17 Scroll down and select from the title list the slide where the hyperlink will jump when it is accessed: **Slide 17, Keyboarding Text for Readability**.

18 Click **OK**.

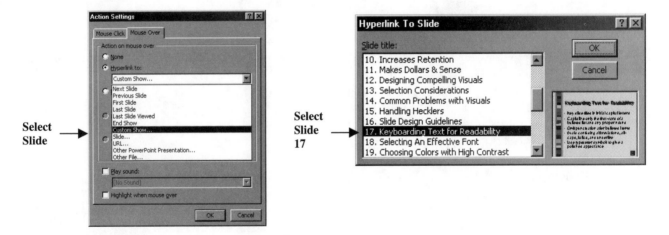

19 Repeat Steps 12–18 to insert the following hyperlinks to specific slides:

Font selection button:	Slide 18, Selecting an Effective Font
Color choice button:	Slide 19, Choosing Colors with High Contrast
Slide orientation button:	Slide 20, Selecting Appropriate Slide Orientation

Create the Return Hyperlinks

20   Display Slide 17 (Keyboarding Text for Readability) in Slide view.

21   Click **Slide Show, Action Buttons**. (Alternately, click **AutoShapes, Action Buttons**).

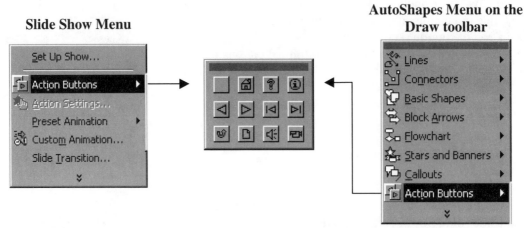

22   Note the (a) ready-made action buttons that depict commonly understood symbols [arrows that refer to next, previous, first, and last slide, information, help, sound, and movies] and (b) a custom button to which your own text or graphics can be added.

23   Select the left arrow **or** the custom button that will remind you to go back to the Summary Slide:

24   Drag to draw the button. When you release the mouse, the Action Settings dialog box appears.

25   Be sure the **Mouse Click** tab is selected.

26   Click the **Hyperlink to** option and the list arrow next to it.

27   Click **Slide**.

28   Scroll down and select from the title list the slide where the hyperlink will jump when it is accessed: **Slide 16, Slide Design Guidelines**.

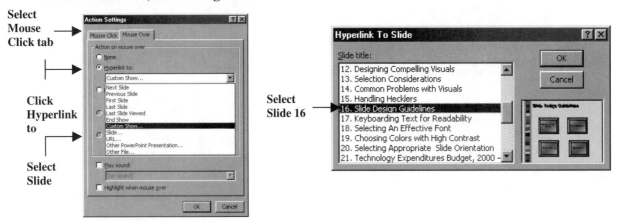

Edit the AutoShape (the Button)

29   Select a fill color, line color, and line style. Consider using a design similar to the button on the summary slide to remind you of the destination.

30   Size the button to achieve a subtle look but large enough that can be clicked conveniently while running the presentation.

FYI

A shortcut for editing an AutoShape is to right click and click **Format, AutoShape**. The tabs allow you to conveniently edit (a) lines and color, (b) size, and (c) position. Specific techniques that can be applied from these menus follow:

Size Tab

1. Input an exact dimension and then compare these values with other AutoShapes to ensure consistency.
2. Input a percentage in the scale section. Click **Lock aspect ratio** to change the height and width proportionally.

Input exact dimensions

Click Lock aspect ratio

Input a percentage to resize an object

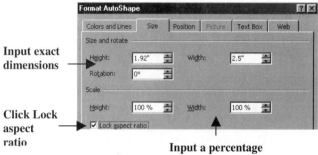

Position Tab

Increase or decrease the horizontal or vertical placement to align an object in a precise location.

Input exact position

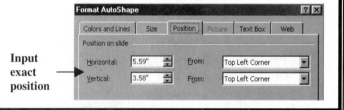

Create the Remaining Buttons Using the Copy Feature to Ensure Consistency

31   Select the hyperlink button and click **Copy**.
32   Display Slide18 (Selecting an Effective Font).
33   Click **Paste** to add the hyperlink button to this slide.
       Note: Because you copied the button, the Action Setting is already set to jump to Slide 16.
34   Paste the hyperlink button on Slide 19 (Choose Colors with High Contrast).
35   Paste the hyperlink button on Slide 20 (Selecting an Appropriate Slide Orientation).

Access the Hyperlinks to Verify Accuracy

36   Display the presentation in the Slide Show view.
37   Click the first hyperlink button (Keyboarding Rules). The slide show should jump to Slide 17 (Keyboarding Text for Readability).
38   Click the return hyperlink on Slide 17. The slide show should jump back to the Summary Slide (Slide 16, Slide Design Guidelines).

Designer's Pointer

A return hyperlink could be omitted from Slide 20 (Selecting an Appropriate Slide Orientation) if the speaker intended to access the hyperlinks in the order presented on the slide. Thus, after discussing Slide 20, the speaker would not return to Slide 16 (Slide Design Guidelines) but would advance directly to the next slide Slide 22 (Photo as a Slide Object), bypassing the hidden slide. However, adding the hyperlink to each button gives the speaker flexibility to adapt the presentation order based on audience. Also, an individual viewing a presentation posted on the Internet could access the hyperlinks in any order and return conveniently to the summary slide.

39 Follow this procedure for editing an action setting if the hyperlink does not jump to the correct slide:

    a.   Right click and click **Hyperlink, Edit Hyperlink**.

    b.   Edit the Action Setting Box by selecting the correct slide from the list.

    PowerPoint 97 Users: Click **Slide Show, Action Settings** to edit the Action Settings dialog box.

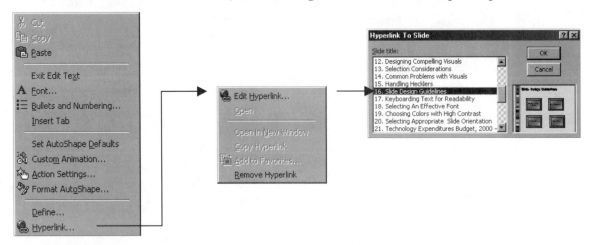

40 Follow the previous procedure to verify the accuracy of the other three hyperlink buttons on the Summary Slide and each return hyperlink to the Summary Slide.

Linking a Chart Created in Excel to a PowerPoint Slide

The linking feature allows managers to update timely information efficiently and conveniently. When current values are input into a notebook file, these changes are reflected automatically in other documents that are linked to this notebook file — e.g., charts in a written report prepared in word processing software and visuals prepared in PowerPoint.

Creating the Notebook File

Directions: To complete this project, you will (a) create a column chart in an Excel notebook based on the data in the notebook, (b) link the chart to a slide in the PowerPoint file **Speak**, and (c) and input a new value and then verify the automatic update of the chart on the PowerPoint slide to reflect the change.

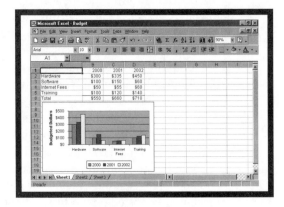

Excel Notebook

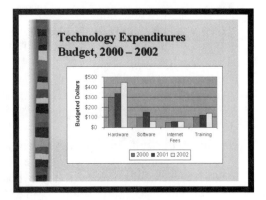

Slide with Chart Linked to Excel Notebook

Create the Notebook File

1 Open Microsoft Excel (Click **Start, Programs, Office 2000, Excel**).

2 Enter the labels and amounts (including the $ signs) shown for each cell.

	A	B	C	D
1		2000	2001	2002
2	Hardware	$300	$335	$450
3	Software	$100	$150	$60
4	Internet Fees	$50	$55	$60
5	Training	$100	$120	$140
6	Total	$550	$660	$710

3 Increase the width of column A:
   a. Position the cell pointer on any cell in column A.
   b. Select **Format**, **Column**, **Width**. Enter **18** and click **Enter**.

4 Highlight cells **B5 to D5** and click the **Borders** icon on the Formatting toolbar.

Borders

Create the Chart

5 Highlight cells **A1 to D5**.
   Note: This range does not include the column totals.

6 Click the **Chart Wizard** button on the Standard toolbar.

Chart Wizard

Respond to the Wizard Prompts to Build the Chart

7 Click **Column** for the Chart Type and **Clustered Column** for the chart sub-type.

8 Click **Next** to confirm the chart type.

9 Click **Next** to confirm the chart source data.

10 Be sure the **Titles** tab is selected and input the label for the Y-axis: **Budgeted Dollars**.
   Note: The items in the X-axis are self-explanatory; therefore, the X-axis label is omitted to keep the chart simple and uncluttered.

Titles tab is selected →

Input label for Y-axis →

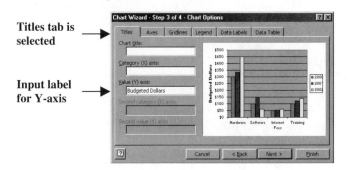

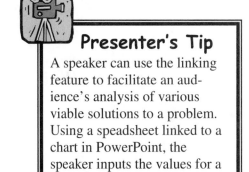

Presenter's Tip

A speaker can use the linking feature to facilitate an audience's analysis of various viable solutions to a problem. Using a speadsheet linked to a chart in PowerPoint, the speaker inputs the values for a specific "what if" analysis and then switches to project the results on a PowerPoint slide.

11 Make sure the **As object in** button is selected.

Select As object in →

12 Click **Finish**.

Format the Chart

13 Make the following changes:

a. Change the font size for the category axis to be **8 points bold** so that the expense categories (hardware, software, Internet fees, and training) will fit horizontally across the X-axis.

b. Move the legend below the column chart.

14 Save the notebook using the file name **Budget**.

15 Minimize Excel and make PowerPoint your active application.

Note: If you minimized PowerPoint when you opened Excel, simply click the PowerPoint bar at the bottom of the screen.

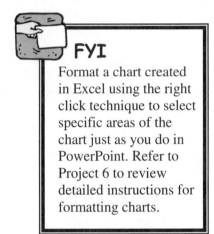

FYI

Format a chart created in Excel using the right click technique to select specific areas of the chart just as you do in PowerPoint. Refer to Project 6 to review detailed instructions for formatting charts.

Copying the Chart from Excel into PowerPoint

16 Select the column chart by pointing and clicking to the outside border of the chart.

Note: Handles appear on the outside border of the chart when the chart area is selected.

Graph Is Selected

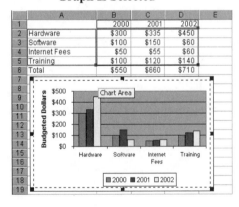

17 Click **Copy**.

18 Minimize PowerPoint and make Excel your active application.

19 Create a new slide to appear after Slide 13 (Selection Considerations). Use the **Chart** AutoLayout.

20 Key the chart title in the slide title placeholder: **Technology Expenditures Budget, 2000 – 2001**.

Note: Refer to the FYI for instructions for formatting this title.

21 Click **once** in the chart placeholder.

Link the Notebook File to the PowerPoint Slide
22   Click **Edit, Paste Special**.

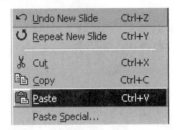

23   Click **Paste Link**.

Click
Paste
Link →

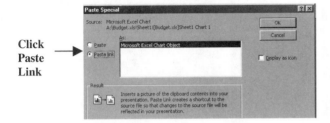

Update the Linked Notebook
24   Click to select the chart on Slide 12 (Technology Expenditures Budget).
25   Right click and click **Linked Worksheet Object, Edit**. The notebook file is displayed automatically.

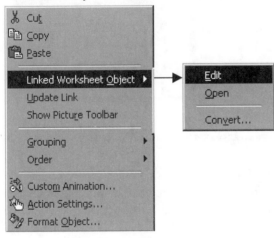

26   Change the cost of training in 2002 to $**500**.
27   Save the file.
28   Return to the PowerPoint slide and note that the chart reflects the new value.

Designer's Pointer

Use special symbols for characters not located on the keyboard to create highly professional slides and handouts and to ensure accuracy when phonetic spelling is needed. Some keystrokes are automatically replaced with special symbols (e.g., common fractions, quotation marks). To insert a symbol, click **Insert, Symbol**. Click the appropriate category and scroll to locate the desired symbol.

En-dash
Use to separate words indicating a duration (May – June or 2000 – 2001)

Em-dash
Use instead of a dash (- -) to indicate an abrupt change in thought or a title (Project 9 — Hyperlinks).

Quotation marks
Use instead of inch (") and foot (').

Fractions
Create ½ and ¼ rather than key the numbers separated by a slash. Special symbols are available for common fractions.

Phonetic spelling
Key José rather than Jose and résumé rather than resume for accuracy.

Other symbols
Use the symbols for ©, ®, ™, ÷, ¶, etc.

FYI
If the link to the notebook file is broken, right click and click **Update Link**.

Other Techniques for Adding Interactivity to Slides

Hidden slides, hyperlinks, and links to notebook files are powerful techniques for making a presentation interactive. In this section, you will create three slides to illustrate simple design techniques that use animation to engage the audience's participation in a presentation.

Interactive Technique 1

Directions: Study the Designer's Pointer that discusses the common content errors illustrated in the original slides. Create the enhanced slide that eliminates these content errors.

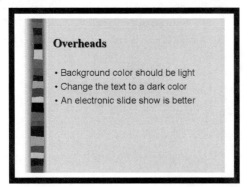
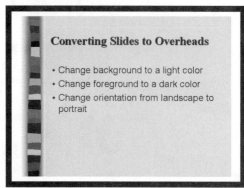

Original Slides

1 Create a new slide to appear after Slide 21 (Selecting Appropriate Slide Orientation). Use the **2-Column Text** AutoLayout.
2 Key the slide title and the bulleted lists shown in the enhanced slide (at right).
   Note: To remove the bullet before the title in each column, click **Format, Bullet**.
   PowerPoint 2000: Click **None**.
   PowerPoint 97:   Click to remove the check in front of **Use a Bullet**.

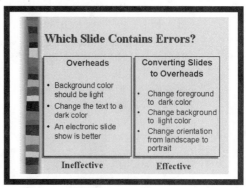

Enhanced Slide

Designer's Pointer

The original slides above violate four important guidelines for writing clear, easy-to-follow slide content:

(1) **Place ideas to be compared on the same slide.** The two original slides should be combined to assist the speaker in leading the audience through an analysis of slide design principles. This goal is difficult to achieve with the information presented on separate slides. Additionally, spreading information out when it should be logically combined leads to slide overload.

(2) **Items in a bulleted list appear together for a similar purpose; therefore, each item in the list must serve the same purpose.** For example, in the original slide, the first and second points are steps in the process of converting slides to overheads. The third item is not a step but appears to be a random fact added to this slide and should be omitted.

(3) **Slide titles should reflect the exact content of the slide in a way that will engage the audience's attention.** The vagueness of the slide titles in the original slides adds to the confusion caused by including an uncommon item in the bulleted list. The revised title, *Converting Slides to Overhead*, previews the slide content and prepares the audience for understanding the process to be discussed.

(4) **Items in a bulleted list should be parallel.** If one item is presented in a different way grammatically, it appears out of place and weakens the emphasis given to each item in the list. The inconsistency may distract the audience's attention from the message. Because the bulleted list describes steps in a process, each step should begin with an action verb (e.g., *change*).

Add a Border to Create a Slide Effect

3 Select both columns of the bulleted list.

4 Click the **Line Color** button on the Draw toolbar and select a color complimentary with the template.

5 Click the **Line Width** button on the Draw toolbar and choose the desired width.

Create Interactive Text Boxes

6 Create a textbox and input the text: **Ineffective**.

7 Format the text box as desired. Be sure to use a font size large enough to be read and a font color with high contrast to the background.

8 Size and position to fit in a balanced format below the left column.

9 Use the Ctrl and drag technique to create a copy of the textbox below the right column.

10 Edit the text in the text box: **Effective**.

Animate

11 Edit the Custom Animation dialog to create the following effects:

Unanimated:	Slide title
1st:	Left column — wipe right
2nd:	Right column — wipe right automatically **0 seconds** after left column
3rd:	Left text box (Ineffective) — wipe down
4th:	Right text box (Effective) — spiral or a similar effect more dramatic than the effect on the left text box

Interactive Technique 2

Directions: Follow the instructions to build Slide 23 that incorporates an interactive technique.

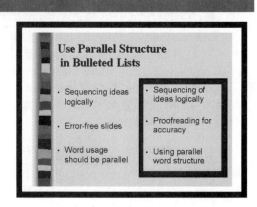

1 Create a new slide to appear after Slide 22 (Which Slide Contains Errors?). Use the **2-Column Text** AutoLayout.

2 Key the slide title and the bulleted lists (shown at right).

Create a Spotlight Box Behind the Right Column

3 Use the rectangle tool to draw a rectangle slightly larger than the right column.

4 Format the rectangle as desired.

5 Position the rectangle directly over the right column and send the rectangle behind the column.

Animate

6 Edit the Custom Animation dialog to create the following effects:

Unanimated:	Slide title
1st:	Left column — wipe right
2nd:	Right column — wipe right automatically **0 seconds** after left column
3rd:	Rectangle — stretch right (forms a spotlight box behind the right column)

Interactive Technique 3

Directions: Follow the instructions to revise Slide 23 to incorporate an alternate interactive technique.

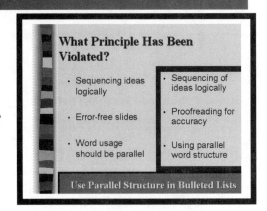

1   Go to the Slide Sorter view and select Slide 23 (Use Parallel Structure in Bulleted Lists).
2   Duplicate Slide 23 to appear as Slide 24 (press Ctrl-D).
3   Display Slide 24 in Normal view.
4   Edit the slide title: **What Principle Has Been Violated?**

Create an Interactive Textbox

5   Create a textbox and input the text: **Use Parallel Structure in Bulleted Lists**.
6   Format the textbox as desired and size to fit across the slide directly below the two columns.

Animate

7   Retain the custom animation copied from the previous slide (slide title, two columns, and rectangle) and animate the text box. Animation should appear as follows:

Unanimated: Slide title
1st: Left column — wipe right
2nd: Right column — wipe right automatically **0 seconds** after left column
3rd: Rectangle — stretch right (forms a spotlight box behind right column)
4th: Text box — spiral or a similar effect more dramatic than wipe right

Inserting Slide Transitions

Directions: Follow the instructions to add slide transitions to the slides created in this project.

1   Display the presentation in Slide Sorter view.
2   Select any slides that do not include a slide transition icon below the slide.
3   Click the **Slide Transition** button on the Slide Sorter toolbar.
4   Select **Wipe Right** effect at a **Fast** speed setting.
5   Click **Apply**.

Printing the Presentation

Directions: Print a copy of the file **Speak** (or **Speakrev**) as an audience handout with six slides per page. The slide should contain the following slides. Slides created in Project 9 are highlighted.

1   Enhanced Title Slide
2   Greatest Fears
3   Effective Speakers
4   Average Presentation Rated
5   Keys to Effective Speaking
6   Why Use Presentation Media
7   Enhances Speaker's Delivery
8   Reduces Speaker Anxiety
9   Helps Speaker Accomplish Goals
10 Increases Retention
11 Makes Dollars and Sense
12 Designing Compelling Visuals
13 Selection Considerations
14 **Technology Expenditures Budget, 2000–2002**

15 Common Problems with Visuals
16 Handling Hecklers
17 **Slide Design Principles**
18 **Keyboarding Text for Readability**
19 **Selecting an Effective Font**
20 **Choosing Colors with High Contrast**
21 **Selecting Appropriate Slide Orientation**
22 **Which Slide Contains Errors?**
23 **Use Parallel Structure in Bulleted Lists**
24 **What Principle Has Been Violated?**
25 Converting Slides to Overheads
26 Photo as Slide Object (slide and photos will vary)
27 The Speaker Is the Star
28 Photo Background (photo will vary)

Project 10
Using the Pack & Go Wizard

Learning Objective

➢ Use the Pack & Go Wizard to pack a presentation on a single diskette so it can be transferred to another computer.

Packing a Presentation

If you enhance your presentations using the techniques presented in this book, likely your PowerPoint file will be too large to fit on a single diskette. Graphics and sound require large amounts of disk space. PowerPoint's Pack and Go Wizard makes packing a presentation simple. The wizard packs all the files and fonts used in the presentation together on as many disks as necessary and later reassembles the files on another computer when the presentation is unpacked. The wizard allows you to include the PowerPoint Viewer if you intend to run your slide show on a computer that doesn't have Microsoft PowerPoint installed.

Using the Pack & Go Wizard

Directions: Follow the instructions to transfer the presentation **Speak** from your hard drive to multiple floppy disks.

Packing the File

1 Make sure you have a sufficient number of **blank**, formatted diskettes. Label the disks with the file name and a number (e.g., Speak #1, Speak #2, Speak #3, etc.) for identification that will be needed during the unpacking process.

2 Be sure the file **Speak** is open.

3 Insert the disk labeled **Speak #1** in the A: drive.

4 Click **File, Pack & Go.**

5 Follow the prompts on the screen to execute the wizard:
   Note: A diagram at the left of the screen outlines the steps in the process. The green square advances to mark the current step being performed.

Click Pack & Go ➡

   Step 1: Start. Click **Next** to advance through the wizard.
   Step 2: Pick files to pack: Provide the **name of the file** you wish to pack. (The computer automatically selects the file open on your desktop.) Click **Next**.
   Step 3: Choose destination. Indicate you wish to pack the file to the **A: drive.** Click **Next**.
   Step 4: Links. Select whether you wish to include links and embed TrueType fonts. Click **Next**.
   Step 5: Viewer. Click in the box before PowerPoint viewer to add the PowerPoint viewer.

   Note: You will not need the PowerPoint viewer files if you are projecting your presentation on a computer with both the viewer and PowerPoint. Thus, the disk space can be conserved by omitting these files.
   Step 6: Finish. Click **Finish**.

6 Insert Speak #2 when the **Please insert another disk** prompt appears. Press **OK**.

7 Repeat the process inserting the disks in numerical sequence. When the process is complete, the following prompt will appear: **Pack & Go has successfully packed your presentation(s)**.

Unpacking a Presentation Saved on Floppy Disks

1 Create a directory on the hard drive where the file will be unpacked. Refer to the FYI feature box for instructions for creating a directory if necessary.

2 Be sure the disk labeled **Speak #1** is in the A: drive.

3 Go to Windows Explorer: Right click and click **Explore**.

4 Double click the **A: drive** (the location of the packed presentation).

5 Double-click **Pngsetup.**

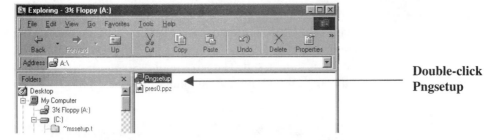

Double-click
Pngsetup

6 Follow the prompts provided by the wizard:

    a. Input the designation directory — the directory where you wish to place the unpacked file (the directory you created in Step 1).

    b. Click **OK**.

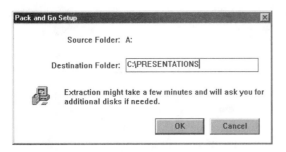

    c. Insert Speak #2 at the **Please insert another disk** prompt.

    d. Continue inserting disks. Be sure to follow the numerical sequence on the labeled disks. A prompt will appear to inform you that the presentation was successfully installed on the hard drive.

    e. Click **Yes** if you wish to view the presentation. Click **No** if you wish to open the presentation so you can edit the file.

FYI

To create a new directory on the hard drive:

1. Go the Windows Explorer: Right click, click **Explore**.

2. Click in the exact location in the Folders column at the left where you wish to add the subdirectory.

3. Click **File, New, Folder**. A folder named "New Folder" appears in the right column.

4. Input a new name for the New Folder:

    — Click to select the New Folder

    — Click **File, Rename**.

    — Input the new name (e.g., Presentations).

INDEX